View From The Veranda

View From The Veranda

The History and Architecture of the Summer Cottages on Mackinac Island

SECOND EDITION

Phil Porter

For John + Pat Many Happy Mackinac Memories

MACKINAC
STATE · HISTORIC · PARKS

Mackinac Island, Michigan

View From the Veranda:
The History and Architecture of the Summer Cottages on Mackinac Island
Second Edition

by Phil Porter
Director
Mackinac State Historic Parks
Mackinac Island, Michigan 49757

Design by Group 230, Lansing
Photographs by John Wooden

© 1981, 2006 Mackinac Island State Park Commission
All rights reserved. First edition 1981
Second edition 2006
Printed in the United States of America

First Printing, 2006   3,000 copies
Second Printing, 2011   3,000 copies

Library of Congress Cataloging-in-Publication Data
Porter, Phil, 1953-
  View from the veranda : the history and architecture of the summer cottages on Mackinac Island / Phil
Porter.--2nd ed.
          p. cm.
  Includes bibliographical references and index.
  ISBN-13: 978-0-911872-41-5 (hardcover)
  ISBN-10: 0-911872-41-8 (hardcover)
  1. Vacation homes--Michigan--Mackinac Island. 2. Mackinac Island (Mich.)--History. 1. Title.
  NA7575.P67 2006
  728.7'209774923--dc22
                                        2006001493

Contents

Introduction

"Bigness, coolness, keen sweeping winds, a view of the broad straits, and far away down Lake Michigan, from everyone of the high, wide windows, soft, cool colors inside and clear spaces, restful to the eye, a few quiet toned pictures, billowy cushions in dainty tints just where you want them, not too many draperies, natural wood furnishings — sleeping apartments as large as the drawing room at home, unexpected little alcoves everywhere, fitted with sleep enticing couches, verandas with hammocks swung across the corners, the cool shadows and deep stillness of the woods just at the back door, the broad, shimmering ever-changing glory of the blue lake in front — this is a Mackinac cottage."

- *Petoskey Daily Resorter*, July 28, 1894

View of Mackinac Island from Round Island, c:1840

For generations Americans have sought pleasant surroundings for summer vacations.

Whether a mountain retreat in the woods, a bubbling hot spring health spa or a fashionable lakeside "watering spot," summer sojourners have scoured the continent to find places to "get away from it all."

The earliest American resorts were those which boasted mineral spring water. Health seekers have long believed in the medicinal use of spring water as a cure-all for most every disease imaginable. As a result, the towns of Stafford Springs, Connecticut; Berkeley Springs, Virginia; and Saratoga Springs, New York were all popular eighteenth-century American resorts for the well-heeled.

By 1850 industrial development and the massive influx of immigrants created unpleasant living conditions in American cities. Coal smoke, machinery noise and crowded quarters, all compounded by summer's heat and humidity, made urban areas uncomfortable for the healthy, and unbearable for the sickly. For relief from these conditions, those who could afford it began to explore resort towns that were developing across the United States and Canada.

If the search for a healthy environment helped establish many American resorts, the effects of the Civil War certainly assured their success. Longing to forget the devastation and human loss of the conflict, post-war Americans passionately sought places where the cares of the world could be forgotten. For emotionally drained survivors, there was a need to escape and, as a result, new resort communities emerged.

The conclusion of the Civil War also saw the beginning of a major transformation in American industry. The almost overnight growth of resort towns was made possible by the development of new technologies, especially in transportation. Between 1870 and 1900 there was a tremendous expansion in railroad and steam navigation service extending to remote areas.

Especially popular in northern climates were resorts that were near water. Affluent easterners would flee the summer heat of Washington, D.C., Boston, and New York City for the New England havens of Nantucket, Massachusetts, Newport, Rhode Island and Kennebunkport, Maine. Their counterparts in the Midwest journeyed to the cool lakes of northern Michigan, Wisconsin and Minnesota. The northern Michigan communities of Petoskey, Harbor Springs, and Charlevoix all became permanent towns because of their attractiveness as summer places. But, of all Midwestern resorts, none enjoyed the rich heritage and widespread popularity of Mackinac Island.

Mackinac Island is located at the juncture of Lakes Huron and Michigan in the Straits of Mackinac. The island is eight miles in circumference with a fine natural harbor on the southern side. Mackinac's rock-covered shore lies beneath impressive bluffs that rise one-hundred and fifty feet above the lake. Because of its hump-backed appearance, native people named the island "Michilimackinac," meaning place of the great turtle. For decades the name was used when referring to the entire straits area. By the middle of the nineteenth century it was shortened to "Mackinac."

Mackinac Island has always been busy in the summer and quiet during the winter. For centuries Ojibwa Indians set up their lodges on the island's shore as they spent the summer months fishing the straits for whitefish and lake trout. In autumn they would return to their traditional hunting grounds.

The Great Lakes fur trade began in the late seventeenth century and generated significant summer activity in the Straits of Mackinac which became a major trans-shipment point for the trade. Established by French merchants and expanded by the British, the straits area fur trade was first centered at St. Ignace, later reestablished on the south side of the straits (present-day Mackinaw City) and eventually moved to Mackinac Island.

During the first thirty-five years of the nineteenth century Mackinac Island was the preeminent summer depot for the upper Great Lakes fur trade. The American Fur Company established its northern department headquarters on the island and every summer thousands of dollars worth of pelts were gathered there and prepared for shipment to eastern markets. Clerks, voyageurs and traders flocked to the island to carry on their business in a flurry of activity that quickly subsided as autumn approached.

Commercial fishing became Mackinac's dominant industry in the 1840s. Like the fur trade, fishing was a summer business. The island docks bustled with activity as small Mackinaw boats delivered fresh whitefish and lake trout to local merchants who salted the catch and packed them into barrels for shipment on the large steamboats to Chicago and Detroit. By 1860 Mackinac Island was the dominant fish processing and shipping center in the upper Great Lakes.

Tourists flocked to Mackinac Island in the years after the Civil War. Midwesterners looking to replace the horrors of war with a romantic and peaceful vacation soon discovered Mackinac's historic charm, scenic beauty and healthy environment. By the 1870s it was apparent that people were no longer coming to Mackinac for furs and fish. Summer fun was now the business of Mackinac.

CHAPTER ONE

The Development of Mackinac Island as a Summer Resort

❦

"As a place of resort during the summer months,
there can be none more desirable — none possessing more attractive
features and health-restoring influences, than this Island of Mackinaw.
The cold, transparent waters — the pure bracing air — the delicious
white fish and trout, posses a strengthing, life-renewing efficacy,
and give to the enervated system of the invalid,
new strength and healthful action."

- *New York Weekly Tribune*, Saturday, July 9, 1853

❦

VIEW OF THE TOWN OF MA KINAW.

Europeans first settled on Mackinac Island during the American Revolution.

Upon assuming command of Fort Michilimackinac, on the south side of the straits in 1779, Lieutenant Governor Patrick Sinclair deemed it indefensible. The simple, wooden-palisaded outpost housed British soldiers and civilians involved in the fur trade.

Sinclair decided that the high bluffs of Mackinac Island would be more secure. Between 1779 and 1781 soldiers and inhabitants moved their belongings and even some buildings to the island. The newly constructed fort housed only the military personnel; civilians established residence below the fort near the harbor.

Following the American Revolution control of the island was juggled between the United States and Great Britain. Finally, the Treaty of Ghent signed in 1814 at the end of the War of 1812 made Mackinac Island the permanent property of the United States.

By 1820 visitors already spoke of the island's beauty and charm. Henry Schoolcraft, the United States Indian agent on Mackinac Island from 1833 to 1841, was captivated by the

At right: Late 19th century tourists visit Sugar Loaf Rock.

island's beauty when he first saw it in 1820. As a student of the natural sciences he took particular interest in the island's geography. He wrote:

Nothing can exceed the beauty of this island. It is a mass of calcareous rock, rising from the bed of Lake Huron, and reaching an elevation of more than three hundred feet above the water. The waters around are purity itself. Some of its cliffs shoot up perpendicularly, and tower in pinnacles like ruinous Gothic steeples. It is cavernous in some places; and in these caverns, the ancient Indians, like those of India, have placed their dead. Portions of the beach are level, and adapted to landing from boats and canoes. The harbor, at its south end, is a little gem.[1]

Throughout the nineteenth century nearly all visitors to Mackinac Island were impressed by its unique limestone formations. Early tourists eagerly visited Sugar Loaf Rock, Devil's Kitchen, Skull Cave, Arch Rock, Lover's Leap and Robinson's Folly. Each site was endowed with its own story of Indian mythology, historic adventure or romance and tragedy. Journalists enthusiastically repeated (and embellished) the stories in newspaper and magazines articles which helped to popularize the island.

Travelers were also fascinated by the island's quaintness and historic charm. Nineteenth-century Americans, eager to visit the nation's historic shrines, soon discovered that Mackinac Island had been a sacred burial ground for American Indians, a reference point for explorers, a fur trade center and a home for the military. Visitors rambled along the old streets of the village following paths used by voyageurs and soldiers, missionaries and fur traders. Tourists enthusiastically inspected the "historic sites" which included British

Landing, the old battlefield and Fort Mackinac. The impressive white stone walls of the fort and the sounds of cannon and bugles provided an air of military grandeur.

The island was a cultural melting pot in which French, English and Indian customs were practiced. Wigwams stood on the beach, Métis boys played in their canoes, foreign languages and accents were heard throughout the village and colorful French-Canadian and Indian garb was proudly worn. When William Cullen Bryant visited the island in 1846 he found it to be peaceful and charming because it was without "improvements." Ironically, his only fear was that because of its cool summer climate it would "become a fashionable watering place, in which case it must yield to the common fate of American villages and improve, as the phrase is."[2]

Early travelers were thrilled when they discovered Mackinac Island's health-restoring environment. Its name was synonymous with salubrity. Visitors enthusiastically sipped water from the cool, natural springs and enjoyed the moderate temperatures. Soon invalids, hay fever sufferers and others with an assortment of ills traveled to the island for comfort. Dr. Hiram R. Mills, Post Surgeon at Fort Mackinac in the 1870s, described the island's location as ideal both "geographically and hydrographically." He claimed the air was pure, buoyant, had more oxygen than warmer climates and was "well stocked with life and health-giving principles." As a result, he recommended it to all who suffered from "a weakly, sickly appearance, low vital powers, feeble pulse, coated tongue, pale or sallow skin, want of appetite, the functions of the various organs of the body inadequately performed and various other conditions."[3]

For most visitors, simply being at Mackinac was conducive to restoring good health.

Whether one was hiking to Arch Rock, touring the historic sites or fishing the straits for lake trout, the activity was invigorating. Visitors were excited to be on the island. Their attitude was positive and their days were refreshing. With their spirits replenished, the battle for physical recovery was all but won.

As the number of visitors increased, transportation service to the island expanded. The development of safe and systematic modes of transportation was crucial to the island's success as a summer resort. Prior to 1875 nearly all visitors to the straits area traveled on board commercial Great Lakes vessels. As early as 1863 the Grand Trunk Steam Line included Mackinac Island on its regular run from Chicago to Sarnia, Ontario. [4] In 1871 the Erie and Western Transportation Company, "The Anchor Line," launched the *China, India* and *Japan*, three identical steamers that served Mackinac Island as a part of their Great Lakes service. The 210 foot steamers carried freight and provided accommodations for up to 150 passengers while plying the lakes at a top speed of twelve miles per hour.[1]

I n 1882 the Detroit and Cleveland Steam Navigation Company began service to Mackinac Island which lasted nearly sixty years. The following year they launched the 300-foot *City of Mackinac,* which joined the *City of Cleveland* in the company's "Mackinac Division."[6] The modest and reliable D&C boats contained about 150 staterooms and made several stops between Cleveland and Mackinac Island. They were described by one long-time island summer resident as the "steady standby that served all of Lake Huron's region."[7]

By 1895 vacationers from Detroit could also take the two luxurious liners of the Northern Steamboat Company, the *North Land* and the *North West.* Their service originated in Buffalo

The 385-foot long steamer North West *had a capacity of 540 passengers.*

and terminated in Duluth. The only stops in between were at Cleveland, Detroit, Mackinac Island, and Sault Ste. Marie, Michigan. The 385-foot sister ships made the run from Detroit to Mackinac in twenty hours and were the first constructed exclusively for passenger travel.[8]

Midwestern railroad companies competed with the steamboat lines for the business of northbound tourists. In 1875 the Grand Rapids and Indiana Railroad completed service to Petoskey. Passengers bound for Mackinac Island boarded small trains that transported them to Crooked Lake. Here they chartered steamboats that took them through the "inland

Michigan Central Railroad promotional brochures featured Mackinac Island as a premier destination that was easily accessible from the nation's growing rail routes.

waterway," a series of lakes and rivers that connected Petoskey to Cheboygan on the Straits of Mackinac, where larger vessels left daily for the island. For those wanting more direct service, the steamer *Music* made regular trips between Petoskey and Mackinac Island. [9]

I n the early 1880s both the Grand Rapids and Indiana and Michigan Central railroads completed service to Mackinaw City. As the nation's railway system expanded, it became possible to board a train in almost any major Midwestern city and arrive at the straits within a day or two. Passenger ferry boat service to Mackinac Island began in the 1880s in order to serve the influx of tourists arriving by train in Mackinaw City.

Early 20th century view of the Grand Hotel.

During the last twenty-five years of the nineteenth century, passenger boat and railroad companies were in fierce competition for tourists traveling to northern Michigan. These companies spent a great deal of time and money promoting the area and publishing pamphlets which extolled the virtues of their line and the places they served. Several transportation companies also made substantial investments in the development of resort facilities – most significantly, in the construction of the Grand Hotel on Mackinac Island.

In 1887 the Detroit and Cleveland Steam Navigation Company and the Grand Rapids and Indiana and Michigan Central railroads formed The Mackinac Island Hotel Company and pooled their funds to build Grand Hotel. Mackinac's smaller hotels simply could not accommodate the ever-increasing number of visitors arriving on the island. The housing shortage prompted the competing transportation companies to join forces and construct the hotel in order to avoid any disruption to their lucrative boat and train businesses. The venture was a great success and the addition of the palatial Grand Hotel established Mackinac Island as northern Michigan's most fashionable resort.

In recognition of the island's growing popularity and in an attempt to preserve this burgeoning resort, the United States government created Mackinac National Park in 1875. This was America's second national park, established just three years after Yellowstone. Senator Thomas W. Ferry of Michigan introduced the bill creating the park in 1873. Ferry had a special interest in the island as it was his birthplace and childhood home. His father, Rev. William M. Ferry, was the superintendent of the island's Protestant mission from 1823 to 1834.

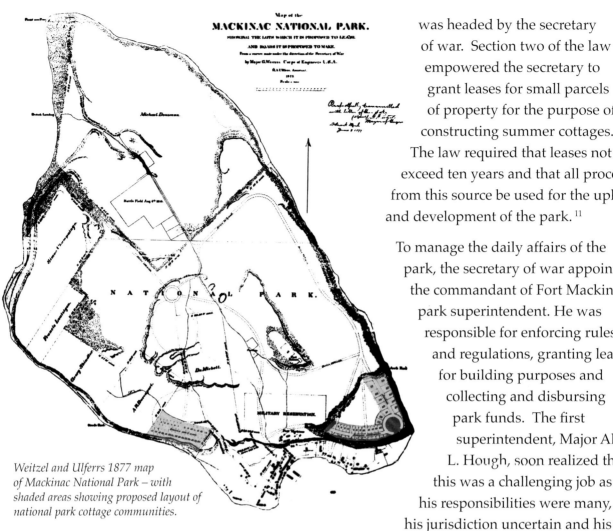

Map of the
MACKINAC NATIONAL PARK.
SHOWING THE LOTS WHICH IT IS PROPOSED TO LEASE.
AND ROADS IT IS PROPOSED TO MAKE.
From a survey made under the direction of the Secretary of War
by Major G. Weitzel Corps of Engineers U.S.A.
H.A. Ulffers, Assistant.
1877
Scale: 1 inch

Weitzel and Ulferrs 1877 map of Mackinac National Park – with shaded areas showing proposed layout of national park cottage communities.

was headed by the secretary of war. Section two of the law empowered the secretary to grant leases for small parcels of property for the purpose of constructing summer cottages. The law required that leases not exceed ten years and that all proceeds from this source be used for the upkeep and development of the park. [11]

To manage the daily affairs of the park, the secretary of war appointed the commandant of Fort Mackinac park superintendent. He was responsible for enforcing rules and regulations, granting leases for building purposes and collecting and disbursing park funds. The first superintendent, Major Alfred L. Hough, soon realized that this was a challenging job as his responsibilities were many, his jurisdiction uncertain and his funds limited.

Senator Ferry's bill proposed that 1000 acres of federal property on the island be set aside as a public park. Only the fort and a small parcel of land surrounding it were kept as a military reservation. In 1875 Congress passed the bill and President U.S. Grant signed it into law. The law stipulated that these lands would be:

> . . . *reserved and withdrawn from settlement, occupancy, or sale under the laws of the United States, and dedicated and set apart as a National Public park or grounds, for health, comfort and pleasure, for the benefit and enjoyment of the people . . .* [10]

As at Yellowstone, the park was placed under the jurisdiction of the War Department, which

A survey was necessary to determine the boundaries of the new park and to establish sites for the building lots. Major Godfrey Weitzel of the U.S. Corps of Engineers in Detroit supervised the project, which was not completed until 1877. His assistant, H.A. Ulffers, conducted the survey and drew a map of the island showing the metes and bounds of park property, proposed roads, and building sites for summer cottages.

To govern the park Weitzel and Hough drew up a list of rules and regulations which Secretary of War Robert T. Lincoln approved in 1875. They protected the charm, character and natural curiosities of the island and established the commandant's authority.

Two companies of United States Army infantry soliders on the Fort Mackinac parade ground, ca. 1890.

The army assigned Fort Mackinac a second company of soldiers to help manage the new park and enforce the rules. Accommodating additional soldiers necessitated physical changes. Over the next few years soldiers built two sets of officers' quarters, a sergeant's quarters, laundress' quarters, powder magazine, commissary and schoolhouse. The commandant was authorized to give extra pay to the men working on these and other projects within the military reservation. But, when he requested the use of military personnel for improvements in the park, the secretary of war told him that money was not appropriated for this purpose and could not be taken from the division's incidental expenses fund.[12] The root of the problem was Congress' unwillingness to use federal monies in the development of public parks.

As a result, the new roads and building lots suggested on the national park map could not be staked or cleared until funds were available. Park properties remained undeveloped for nearly ten years and prospective summer cottagers became frustrated in their attempts to lease lots within the park. Their complaints seemed to fall on deaf ears and they began to wonder if their dreams of summer residence on the island would ever become a reality.

CHAPTER TWO
Origins of the Cottage Communities

"The rage for investment in lands was now manifest
in every visitor that came from the East to the West . . .
Among other plans, an opinion arose that Michilimackinac
must become a favorite watering place, or refuge
for the opulent and invalids during the summer,
and lots were eagerly bought up from Detroit and Chicago."

- Henry R. Schoolcraft, *Personal Memoirs*, August 1835

The demand for tourist accommodations grew with Mackinac's increasing popularity. Prior to the Civil War the Mission House (1840s), Island House (1852) and Lake View House (1858) provided more than enough rooms to satisfy island visitors.

The post-war tourism boom, however, prompted the construction of additional hotels and boarding houses which accommodated the needs of the casual visitor but fell short of satisfying those who wanted to establish summer roots on the island. For these vacationers, nothing less than a summer cottage would satisfy their desire for a home at Mackinac.

For nearly as long as tourists have been coming to Mackinac Island, there has been a desire to build summer homes. In 1835 U.S. Secretary of War Lewis Cass purchased a lot on the island and left instructions to "have buildings erected on it sufficient for the summer residence of four families."[1] Fourteen years later W.B. Ogden of Chicago requested a building lot in the military reserve on the bluff overlooking the town and harbor.[2] Although Ogden's request was turned down, it foreshadowed the growing interest in using government lands for this purpose. The creation of Mackinac National Park stimulated new enthusiasm for establishing summer residences on federal property. Yet, despite the growing demand, park lots could not be leased until they were properly surveyed and staked.

The island homes that were available for summer use were located on private property in the village and were rented long before the

Gurdon S. Hubbard

season began. Yearly rental fees in the 1880s were between $50 and $100 for an unfurnished home and $200 and $350 for a furnished home.[3] Throughout this period the demand for summer homes remained greater than the supply. One man who was prepared to take advantage of this situation was Gurdon S. Hubbard.

Hubbard was born in Windsor, Vermont in 1802 and came to Mackinac Island in 1818 as a clerk for the American Fur Company. In 1828 he bought out the company's interest in Illinois and began a long career as an independent businessman. Hubbard, a pioneer in the development of Chicago, incorporated the Chicago Hydraulic Company, owned a meat packing business and formed the Eagle Steamship Line. He helped organize the Chicago Board of Trade, was director of the Chicago branch of the State Bank of Illinois and served as a representative in the Illinois General Assembly from 1832 to 1833.[4] Although he moved to Chicago, Hubbard remained fond of Mackinac Island. In 1855 he purchased a large portion of the eighty-acre

Gurdon Hubbard on the front porch of his cottage The Lilacs *in 1870. (Mrs. Mack Ernster)*

Ambrose Davenport farm on the southern bluff of the island overlooking the Straits of Mackinac. Here he built a small cottage around 1870 which he named "The Lilacs."

For all of his hard work and ambition Gurdon Hubbard was soon to suffer tragic setbacks in his business ventures. In 1868 his packing house was destroyed by fire and the company folded. In the same decade both the *Superior* and *Lady Elgin* of the Eagle Line were lost to maritime accidents. The Chicago fire of 1871 destroyed his remaining property and businesses and left him financially crippled.[5] One of his few remaining assets was his old farm and new cottage on Mackinac Island.

Because of his financial problems, and despite his increasing age and failing eyesight,

Hubbard decided to develop his property and take advantage of the growing demand for summer lodging on Mackinac Island. With funds borrowed from wealthy Chicago associates, the eighty-year-old businessman had his land surveyed and platted in 1882. He hoped to establish a fashionable resort hotel and an exclusive cottage community. The hotel never materialized, but the cottage community became an immediate success.

Hubbard divided his property into fourteen blocks that contained one hundred and thirty-two building lots. He named his development "Hubbard's Annex to the Mackinac National Park;" today it is simply known as "The Annex." Hubbard's plan was to create a club-like resort community where cottage ownership would include access to the community's parks and

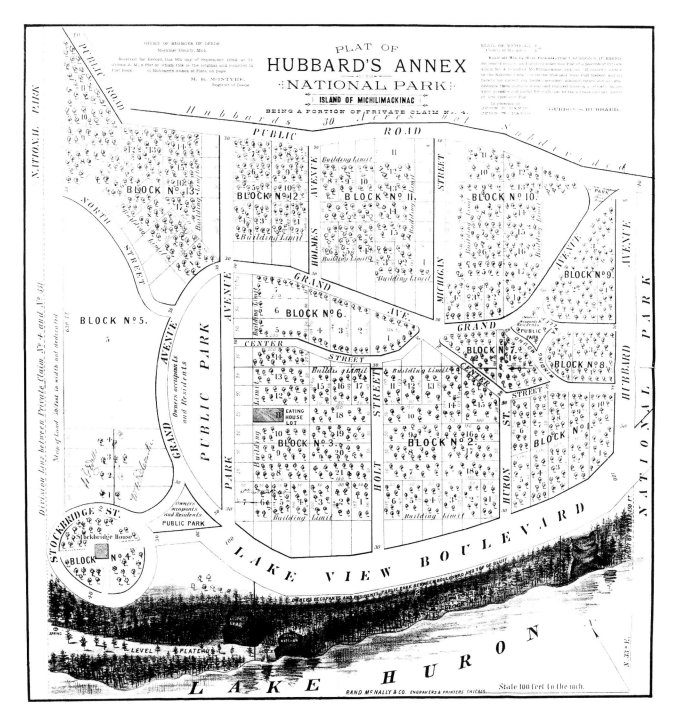

the use of a communal dining and guest house. Hubbard was an able promoter and shared his scheme with a wide network of friends and interested parties throughout the Midwest. His timing was excellent as he capitalized on the growing demand for building lots, and did so just three years before the national park lots became available.

For nearly ten years after Mackinac National Park was established in 1875 the proposed building lots in Mackinac National Park remained undeveloped because funding had not been provided to have the lots surveyed and staked. Park superintendents received dozens of inquiries and requests for building lots but had nothing to offer to frustrated applicants. In November 1875 Major Alfred Hough received the first three requests

Building Lots

Island of Mackinac, Mich.

FOR SALE.

THOSE who intend to build Summer Residences on Mackinac Island, will find the most desirable Lots, at very reasonable prices, on the western part of the Island, around the rock known as "Lover's Leap" and above the caves known as the "Devil's Kitchen."

An 80-acre lot has been neatly laid out and until the Colony, already started, is as large as is desired, lots will be sold on very advantageous terms to the purchaser.

The view from this bluff is the finest on the Island, overlooking the entrance to Lake Michigan with its numerous Islands and Light-Houses, and in full view of St. Ignace and Mackinaw City.

For Particulars, address

GURDON S. HUBBARD,

243 Locust Street,   CHICAGO.

Opposite: Plat map of Hubbard's Annex to the Mackinac National Park.

Above: An 1882 advertisement for building lots in Hubbard's Annex.

for leases. One of the applicants was Francis B. Stockbridge, a former representative and senator in the Michigan legislature who was engaged in lumbering in the state's upper peninsula. Both he and his business partner, O.W. Johnson, requested lots on the south front of the island, east of the military reserve.[6] Hough immediately informed his supervisors of the applicants and mentioned that the individuals were eager to build by the following spring. Hough was anxious to please the applicants and recommended the leases be made.[7] He received no reply from headquarters and was powerless to help.

By 1882 Captain Edwin Sellers had received seven lease applications and sent paperwork to the interested parties for completion. With no opportunity to construct, the applicants refused to execute the leases.[8] Senator Thomas Ferry,

concerned about the implementation of the law he had sponsored, wrote Secretary of War Robert Lincoln in August of 1882 requesting information about the leasing of the lots. Lincoln told him that it would cost at least $2,500 to survey and stake the lots and that such funds would be available only if appropriated by Congress.[9]

In 1884 companies "E" and "K" of the Twenty-Third Regiment of Infantry were assigned to Fort Mackinac. Among the new group of commissioned officers was Lieutenant Calvin D. Cowles, a trained surveyor. When the lease applicants learned of Cowles' abilities, new pressures were applied to the secretary of war. On August 14, 1884 Illinois congressman William Springer wrote the secretary saying:

> *I am informed that there is a competent surveyor connected with the military post at Fort Mackinac, and that he could make a plat of the National Park, or that part suitable for residences, without expense to the government, if furnished by the department with the necessary instruments. There are several families who desire to erect cottages for next season and only await the surveying and platting of that part of the park on the bluff overlooking the east end of the village.[10]*

Cowles seemed to be the answer to the applicants' problems. Springer's letter to Secretary Lincoln was followed by one from the new park superintendent, Captain George Brady. Brady confirmed that Lieutenant Cowles would be able to make the survey if the army could supply a theodolite, a leveling staff, and a surveyor's chain.[11] The instruments were provided and on October 30, 1884 the War Department directed that the national park building lots be properly surveyed.[12]

Cowles was assisted by Lieutenant Benjamin Morse who surveyed the "West Bluff" lots

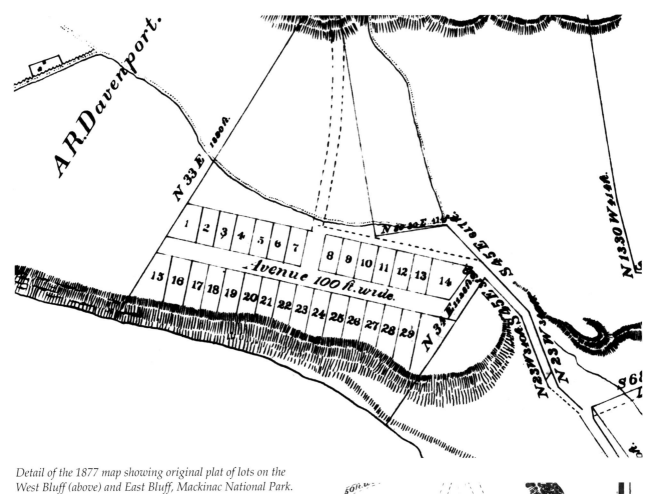

Detail of the 1877 map showing original plat of lots on the West Bluff (above) and East Bluff, Mackinac National Park.

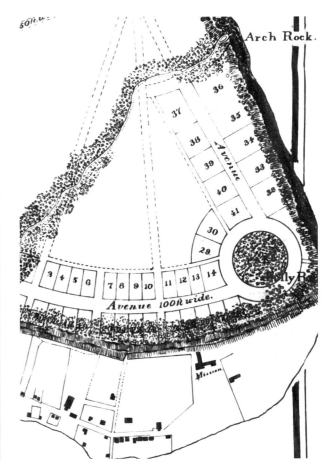

while Cowles worked on those on the "East Bluff." By December 1884 they completed their work. After waiting nearly ten years, interested parties could now lease National Park property with confidence. Further, the superintendent could begin collecting rent that would be used for park improvements. And, those individuals who for so long had dreamed of owning a summer cottage on the picturesque limestone bluffs could begin construction as soon as the winter season passed.

L easing property and building a cottage in the national park was more complicated than in the Annex as a result of having the federal government as landlord. Park lessees had to follow several rules and regulations concerning the administration of the leases and the construction of the cottages. A lease form was drawn up, and in April of 1885 Captain

Brady contracted with the Detroit Free Press Co. to do the printing. Applicants were sent four copies which they were to sign and return to the superintendent. All four copies were forwarded to the secretary of war through the quartermaster general's office. If the lease was approved, the secretary returned three copies and kept one. The superintendent returned one to the lessee, sent one to the secretary of the interior and kept one at Fort Mackinac.[13]

The lots were priced at $25, $15, and $10 per year. The front lots with the choicest views commanded the highest price. The term of the lease was ten years, at the end of which time all improvements were to become the property of the government. Many lessees balked at this stipulation. The clause eventually was deleted and renters were given the opportunity to renew their leases upon expiration.

Lessees were also required to send building plans and state the minimum cost of constructing their cottages. The plans had to be approved by the superintendent before construction could begin. They were submitted in many forms including rough sketches, blueprints, and even photographs. Quite often this matter was settled informally by the superintendent and the building contractor. Park rules stated that the cottages were to be constructed at not less than a stated cost. This price frequently changed. In 1886 the cost was set at $800, within two years it rose to $1,500 and by 1889 lessees were required to spend at least $2,000 on their new cottage.[14] Cottages had to be constructed within one year after the lease was issued. Failure to do so resulted in forfeiture of the lease.

Applicants were also required to furnish letters of recommendation. Captain Greenleaf Goodale stated that, "The government desires tenants only of the highest character as good citizens and neighbors."[15] Applicants, of

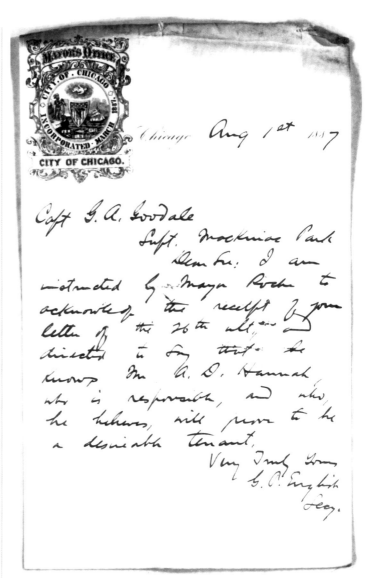

Letter from the office of Chicago Mayor John A. Roche recommending Alexander Hannah as a "desirable tenant" for Mackinac National Park.

course, solicited support from their most influential friends. Mr. A.D. Hannah listed the mayor of Chicago as a reference.[16] John Hoagland thought that a military connection might be useful, and he asked General J. D. Bingham, as assistant quartermaster general, to send a letter in his behalf.[17]

To many, these rules and regulations seemed like bureaucratic busy work. Their purpose, however, was to insure the integrity of the cottagers and the quality of their buildings. And, despite the paperwork and inconvenience, a constant demand for the lots remained.

CHAPTER THREE

Establishment and Growth of the Cottage Communities

"Any number of favorable locations can be obtained
upon which to put the cottages which will surely be built
from year to year and Mackinac Island certainly has
a bright future ahead of it as a place of summer residence."

- *Petoskey Daily Resorter*, August 13, 1891

West Bluff

In 1882 the East Bluff, West Bluff, and the Annex were little more than cedar-covered cliffs overlooking the Straits of Mackinac. Within ten years each was a well-established cottage community inhabited by prominent and wealthy families from Michigan and the Midwest. The Annex, supported by its own resort association, grew quickly while the East and West Bluffs began later and more slowly.

Gurdon Hubbard was in his eighties and nearly blind when he sold his first lot in 1883. For his community to develop in the ways that he planned,

Hubbard needed the support of others. The first Annex cottagers shared his fondness for a communal association and provided the necessary assistance.

During the spring and summer of 1883 eight families constructed cottages in the Annex. They were all situated around the commons which was the largest of the community's parks. The platted lots were small, only about fifty feet wide and one hundred feet long. As a result, most cottagers purchased several lots to accommodate their cottage, barns, corrals and yards.

Hubbard, along with the seven new cottagers, formed the "Mackinac Island Resort Association." Five of the association's members — Hezekiah Wells, William McCourtie, Frank Clark, Theodore Sheldon and Francis Stockbridge — were wealthy Kalamazoo residents who called themselves the "Wah-Cheo Club," a name probably derived from the popular "Achoo Clubs" formed by hay fever sufferers of the period.[1] The other new members of the association were Edwin Street of Grand Rapids and O.W. Johnson of Racine, Wisconsin. Johnson and Stockbridge had been trying to build island cottages since 1875 and, having been turned down by the national park, were delighted to be able to build in the Annex.

The community grew rapidly and by 1886 the resort association boasted sixteen members. Among the newer residents were William Stuart, a law partner of Edwin Street, and George Stockbridge, nephew of Francis. Most of the cottagers came from Kalamazoo and Grand Rapids but other cities, including Detroit and Harbor Springs, Michigan, and New Orleans, were also represented. Officers were elected and the small group began to organize its communal affairs.

The activities of the early Annex cottagers centered around the Eating House which served as a central dining hall and hotel for their guests. To avoid the drudgery of preparing meals and to lessen the possibilities of kitchen fires, all meals were prepared and served in this one location. In the 1880s the association hired G.W. Dickenson, landlord of the Emmet House in Harbor Springs, to oversee the operation of the Eating House.[2]

Across the street from the Eating House was the Annex commons. A large bandstand stood in the middle and was the scene of small concerts and informal gatherings.[3] The association built tennis courts on the north side, and a narrow drive surrounding the commons.

All of the new cottages were built near the commons with the exception of those owned by Hugh McCurdy and the Episcopal Church of Michigan. McCurdy, a resident of Corunna, Michigan, was a prominent probate court judge and one of the highest ranking members of the Masonic Order in the country. The Grand Hotel chose McCurdy to dedicate the guest register

Above: Hezekiah Wells cottage nearing completion in 1883 (Clarke Historical Library, Central Michigan University).

Below: Detail of the Hubbard's Annex plat map showing the Eating House and commons.

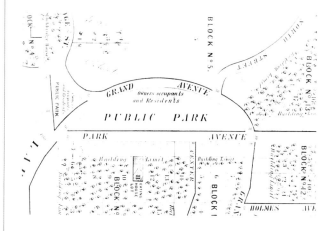

on July 1, 1887. In 1885 the Episcopal Diocese of Michigan built a summer cottage for Reverend Samuel Harris, bishop of Detroit. Both this cottage and McCurdy's were built near the national park's West Bluff and overlooked the Straits of Mackinac.

Above: Annex cottage constructed by the Episcopal Diocese of Michigan in 1885 for Bishop Samuel Harris.

Right: Soldiers pose with Annex residents in front of the Eating House in August 1885.

Hugh McCurdy

Cottagers of
The Annex

William J. Stuart

Francis Stockbridge

Hezekiah G. Wells

Charles W. Caskey built most of these early Annex cottages and the Eating House. Caskey was a native of Allegan, Michigan, where he began his construction business. In the summer of 1880 he traveled to northern Michigan to build a cottage for E.H. Pope in the resort town of Wequetonsing. Returning the following summer, he established permanent residence in Harbor Springs to take advantage of the boom in resort construction.[4] Within a few years he had a prosperous and thriving business building cottages in Wequetonsing, Harbor Springs, Harbor Point, Petoskey and Bay View.

His speed as a builder was well known throughout northern Michigan. When he

constructed his own house in Harbor Springs in 1882, he finished all of the carpentry work in less than one week.[5] His reputation as a qualified and competent worker soon spread to Mackinac Island where he captured the attention of Annex Resort Association members.

Caskey soon fell in love with Mackinac Island, and in 1884 he built his own cottage on the northeast corner of the Annex commons. Caskey and his family enjoyed their summer home for many years. In 1885 he invested in the growing community by building two small cottages which he hoped to sell or lease. He sold one to John S. Belden and leased the other to Dr. L.L. McArthur, both of Chicago.[6]

Charles W. Caskey (Mrs. Ruth Sater)

All of Caskey's materials and supplies had to come from the mainland. Because Harbor Springs was a day's journey from the island, he established a mill and warehouse in neighboring St. Ignace. During the winter and early spring he hauled his supplies across the frozen lake. In the summer, however, all of his freight was carried by steamer. Because of the volume of work that he was doing on the island, he decided to provide his own transportation. In the late 1880s his steamers *A.C. Van Raalte* and *Lou C. Cummings* plied the straits carrying lumber for his cottages.[7]

Caskey took on his most ambitious project when he constructed Grand Hotel in 1887. The ambitious contractor confirmed his reputation as a rapid builder with the hotel project. Using a crew of three hundred men and 1,500,000 feet of lumber, Caskey constructed Grand Hotel in less than four months. His work on the hotel made him a wealthy man, and he began to pursue new business ventures. He invested part of his earnings in the growing resort town of Petoskey, where he built a planing mill, furniture factory and, in 1895, the Imperial Hotel. The construction and management of the Imperial required Caskey's full attention, and he was forced to sell his island cottage and move to Petoskey.[8]

The club-like atmosphere of the Annex flourished as long as its residents were close friends and eager for this type of communal resort life. As new cottages were built and old ones transferred to new hands, these co-operative arrangements faltered. By 1896 five of the original eight cottagers were gone. The association was especially hurt by the loss of Gurdon Hubbard and Francis Stockbridge. Hubbard, who was responsible for developing and nurturing the community's unique character, died in 1886, at the age of 84. With his death the colony lost the strongest supporter of its communal activities. In 1887 Stockbridge was elected to the United States Senate and decided to sell his cottage the following year. He had been president of the association since it was formed, and his leadership was sorely missed. Also gone

Early 20th century views of East Bluff (above) and West Bluff.

Phoebe Gehr cottage, East Bluff

were O. W. Johnson, Hezekiah Wells and Theodore Sheldon, the association's long-time treasurer.[9] By the turn of the century the resort association was disbanded and the Eating House was no longer in use.[10]

The Annex was a small but well developed community of eleven cottages before the first house was built in the national park. The Annex community grew quickly because of the strong leadership of Gurdon Hubbard and the friendship of the early cottagers. The east and west bluffs developed slowly because of government delays and confusion and uncertainty regarding leases.

In 1885 eleven lots were leased in the park and three cottages were constructed, all on the East Bluff. During the summer Chicagoans Phoebe Gehr and Charlotte Warren hired Caskey to build summer homes on lots twenty-one and twenty-two respectively. Each cottage was built at a cost of about $1,000.[11] John Atkinson of Detroit had his cottage erected on lot seventeen during the fall. A. G. Couchois, a local builder, constructed the cottage at a cost of about $2,000.[12]

The following year William Westover of Bay City, Michigan built the first summer home on the West Bluff. In 1887 Alexander Hannah and David Hogg erected twin cottages next door to Westover. Hannah and Hogg owned a large

John Atkinson cottage, East Bluff

distillery firm in Chicago. Their small, yellow cottages were identical except that one had blue trim and the other had red.[13]

Although twenty-three leases had been taken between 1885 and 1888, only seven cottages were erected. Several lessees forfeited their leases because they failed to build within one year. To insure the sincerity of the lease applicants' desire to build, park superintendent Captain Greenleaf A. Goodale suggested that two years rent be prepaid instead of one. He pointed out that the additional charge would probably not discourage lessees and, in case of failure to build, would increase the park fund.[14]

His proposal was approved by the quartermaster general in January of 1888.

Despite a slow beginning, Goodale believed the bluff communities would prosper. He expressed the view, "As the healthfulness of this island and its advantages for a summer residence become generally known, I anticipate a large increase in the demand for park lots."[15] His words were prophetic. Between 1888 and 1893 fourteen cottages were erected on each bluff.

The impetus behind the new surge in growth was the establishment of the Grand Hotel in 1887. Construction of the expansive and elegant Grand Hotel not only changed the island's landscape but also

Frank Clark's Annex cottage Rock-Lawn, *so named, the owner said, "because it is a continual struggle between the rocks and the lawn to see which will beat." (Mrs. Clemens Gunn)*

transformed Mackinac Island from a merely popular vacation spot into the most fashionable resort in the upper Great Lakes. Demand for cottage property soared as prospective summer residents clamored to be a part of this toney new resort. As the hotel's first season came to a close, there was a new feeling of confidence about the island's future. The *St. Ignace News* reported: "Appearances indicate that Mackinac Island as a summer resort is yet in its swaddling cloths, and that next year and the years to come will see many more health and pleasure seekers there than ever before."[16]

Among the new residents on the West Bluff in 1888 and 1889 were four who had previously lived in the Annex. George Stockbridge and Frank Clark of Kalamazoo built at the top of the bluff on lots fifteen and sixteen. For five years Clark maintained two island cottages. It is uncertain which cottage he lived in during this period, but in 1893 he sold his bluff home and lived

exclusively in the Annex. Both men hired a Kalamazoo builder, Edwin Zander, to construct their cottages.[17] The choice of Zander was probably due to the fact that the current building spree had employed all the local contractors. William Hughart and Thomas O'Brien had rented in the Annex before building on the West Bluff near the Grand Hotel. Both men were natives of Grand Rapids, where Hughart was president of the Grand Rapids and Indiana Railroad and O'Brien was the firm's lawyer.

The West Bluff also became home for Delos Blodgett and E. Crofton Fox, successful lumbermen from Grand Rapids. They were next-door neighbors until the death of Blodgett's first wife in 1892, when he gave the cottage to his daughter Susan Lowe. Blodgett remarried and, in the following year, purchased Frank Clark's West Bluff cottage for $8,500.[18]

The island was a popular resort for wealthy Chicago meat packers. The Armours, Swifts, and Cudahys were all frequent guests at Grand

Above: Carpenters completing Frank Clark's West Bluff cottage in 1888. Below: Five years later Delos Blodgett purchased and substantially enlarged and remodeled the Clark cottage. The rear section of the original house can be seen to the left.

The Alexander Hannah barn on the back lot behind his West Bluff cottage.

Hotel. In 1888 John Cudahy built a magnificent $5,000 cottage on lot twenty-five of the West Bluff. His brothers Michael and Edward also owned summer homes on the island.

By the late 1880s it was apparent that the front lots on the bluffs were the only ones considered desirable for cottage sites. In fact, the road separating the two tiers of lots on the West Bluff was not cut until 1887, and then only twenty-five feet wide rather than the proposed one hundred feet.[19] The new road made the back lots available, but by 1889 none had been leased.

For a number of years park residents maintained stables on their cottage lots. The earliest barns were constructed in 1888 by George Stockbridge, Eva Wheeler, Alexander Hannah and Walter Newberry on the West Bluff and Henry Duffield

and John Owen on the East Bluff. Most of the West Bluff cottage lots were small and the stables were uncomfortably close to the residences. As a result, several cottagers petitioned the park superintendent for permission to lease back lots for barns and corrals. Captain Goodale supported their request and explained to the quartermaster general that the rear lots were undesirable as cottage sites and that the presence of stables would not be offensive to the other residents.[20] Leases were approved and John Cudahy and Delos Blodgett built the first back-lot barn behind their West Bluff cottages in the fall of 1891. Two years later the superintendent leased back lots to five other West Bluff residents with the provision, "Upon expiration of leases, the stables are to be removed if lots are desired for residence purposes . . . "[21] Within a year all five cottagers either moved barns from their

Matt Elliott's crew nearing completion of R.S. Taylor's East Bluff cottage Restview, *in 1891 (Mary Truscott)*

front lots or constructed new barns on back lots behind their cottages.

The East Bluff experienced its construction surge between 1890 and 1892, when ten new homes were built. At least half of the new cottages were built by local contractor Mathias Elliott. Elliott constructed homes for R. S. Taylor and Henry Freeman of Fort Wayne, Indiana; H. L. Jenness of Detroit; T. F. Spangler of Zanesville, Ohio; and John Batten of Chicago. Elliott's modest cottages represented a variety of styles and usually cost about $1,500.[22] Rev. Meade C. Williams of Princeton, Illinois also built a cottage on the East Bluff. Williams, an ardent student of Mackinac history, published *Early Mackinac, The Fairy Island* in 1897. He was active in community affairs and was instrumental in the preservation of the island's Mission Church beginning in 1895.

Some of the larger building lots on the East Bluff were divided in order to keep up with the increasing demand. In 1888 lots fifteen and sixteen were made into four parcels. Three years later lot twenty-eight and one-half was created when R.S. Taylor, owner of a cottage on lot twenty-eight, petitioned the Secretary of War to make excess land on the east side of his lot available to his friend Edward A. Gott. In 1892 authority was given to subdivide lots 33, 34, 35 and 36 into eight parcels.[23] Lots thirteen and one-half and fourteen and one-half were added at the top of the East Bluff by the Mackinac Island State Park Commission in the late 1890s.

The success of the bluff communities meant more work for the park superintendent. His responsibilities included issuing leases, checking building plans, approving building sites and

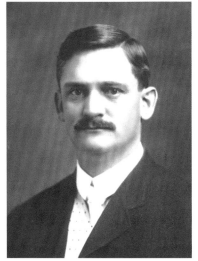

William Hitchcock

Louisa Waldron

Mary E. Walsh

Milton Tootle, Jr.

Meade C. Williams

enforcing rules and regulations. Lessees, who usually lived a great distance from Mackinac Island in the off season, relied on the superintendent for assistance with construction projects. Superintendents reported on building progress, recommended contractors, brokered issues with other lessees and even hired caretakers. Volumes of letters were exchanged and each step was carefully monitored and duly recorded.

The superintendent was also responsible for collecting and disbursing funds. In 1885 Captain George K. Brady established a checking account with the Detroit National Bank.[24] During the first year $275 was raised. The only park improvement that year was the construction of a set of stairs leading to the East Bluff costing $99.50.[25] By 1895 over $7,000 had been raised through lease fees. Most of the money was used for building and maintaining roads in the park. These funds also paid for the construction of an observation tower at Fort Holmes, printing and painting signs, building benches and clerical labor.[26] The park's income was never sufficient to meet all of its expenses. To bolster its funds the government offered military reservation land for public sale on neighboring Bois Blanc Island. The sale was only moderately successful because the land was not particularly attractive to investors or settlers. By 1888 the park had received $1,973.98 from the sale of this property.[27]

William Amberg

Cottagers of The West Bluff

Thomas J. O'Brien

Thomas White

Delos Blodgett

John Cudahy

With all of his other responsibilities, the superintendent also had to police the park grounds. This meant keeping a watchful eye on the cottages when they were vacant. Major Edwin Coates must have been particularly embarrassed when several soldiers from his command were caught breaking into island cottages. Privates William Stugard, Daniel Dean, Henry Phillips and Harvey Wagner of Company "D," 19th Infantry were convicted and incarcerated in the state prison at Marquette, Michigan.[28]

The island cottage communities which began in a modest and tentative fashion bloomed into opulence as the twentieth century approached.

By the mid-1890s nearly every choice lot was the site of a summer home and many residents, eager to follow the opulent lead set by Grand Hotel, began a period of dramatic remodeling. During the decade and through the turn of the century nearly a dozen homes which were no more than ten years old were substantially altered or torn down and replaced with larger and more ornate cottages. When he moved back to the Annex, Frank Clark enlarged and improved his cottage by adding a third floor and a dramatic new facade with a sweeping veranda. Across the commons, Michael Cudahy bought the Francis Stockbridge house in 1889 and remodeled it into one of the largest cottages on the island.

On the East Bluff Henry Duffield, E. P. Barnard, Charles Bowen and Milton Tootle made extensive improvements to their cottages. Duffield added a dramatic lighthouse-style tower to his main facade while, next door, Barnard remodeled and enlarged his simple, cross-gabled home into an impressive Shingle Style cottage. Bowen purchased Charlotte Warren's cottage and expanded the simple home into a large double house connected by a multi-columned porch. Milton Tootle transformed George Smith's non-descript, four-square home into a stunning Neo-Classical Revival mansion.

Architect Asbury W. Buckley designed most of the remodeled cottages on the West Bluff. Originally from Kalamazoo, Buckley later moved to Chicago and provided architectural services to several island cottagers from the Windy City including distillery partners Alexander Hannah and David Hogg. Buckley converted their small twin cottages into large and fashionable Queen Anne-style homes in the early 1890s. Hannah's new cottage incorporated his old building while Hogg moved his original house and had an entirely new cottage erected. Next door, Chicagoan William Amberg followed suit and hired Buckley to turn his newly purchased cottage into an imposing wooden castle. The German-born Amberg proudly named his new home "Inselheim" – Island Home. When Edward Pitkin of Chicago bought George Stockbridge's cottage in 1893, he hired Buckley to redesign it. Eight years later H. H. Hanna bought the cottage and promptly hired Buckley to completely redesign the cottage once again. In at least one instance Buckley served as general contractor as well as architect. When Colonel Henry Davis had his Annex home built in 1893, Buckley did everything from drawing the blueprints to ordering the lumber.[29]

While island cottagers kept busy expanding and improving their cottages in the early 1890s, the War Department pondered the fate of Fort Mackinac. The obsolete fort had long outlived its military importance and, at a cost of $50,000 per year, was an expensive tool for managing Mackinac National Park. In 1894 the army decided to abandon Fort Mackinac and on October 9 most of the troops left the island outpost; only Lieutenant Woodbridge Geary and 11 soldiers stayed behind until the government decided what to do with the fort and park.

Cottagers, residents and visitors were all saddened by the abandonment of the fort, which was the last living link with the island's past. Of more immediate concern was the question of what was to be done with park lands. The cottagers appreciated the efficient administration provided by the military, and were not anxious for their removal. Nor were they pleased with the alternatives suggested by Secretary of War Daniel Lamont. Lamont believed that the national park had become a summer resort for the wealthy, and that the government should no longer be responsible for its upkeep. He suggested that the government sell all park lands except for the fort, which should be retained as a memorial to the early history of the region.[30]

Fearing that the sale of park lands would ruin the unique character of the island, concerned citizens enlisted the support of Michigan U.S. Senator James McMillan. McMillan pursued the suggestion of transferring the park and fort to the State of Michigan for use as a state park. McMillan was an able politician, and he successfully gained the support of the War Department, the senate committee on public buildings and grounds and Michigan Governor John T. Rich.[31] On March 2, 1895 Congress passed legislation transferring the properties to the State of Michigan.

Milton Tootle, Jr. cottage, East Bluff

The Michigan legislature created the Mackinac Island State Park Commission to manage the affairs of Michigan's first state park. Governor Rich appointed the members of the commission, which included Thomas Ferry, who sponsored the national park legislation twenty years earlier. Ferry was elected commission president at the board's first meeting held on July 11, 1895 at Grand Hotel.[32] The commission received no state appropriation to pay for park maintenance. As a result, they voted to raise cottage lot rentals to $100 for the front lots and $60 for rear lots. Two years later the price of the rear lots was dropped to $30.

In May of 1896, the commission hired Homer L. Thayer of Lansing as the first superintendent of the state park. Thayer was paid $800 a year and provided with a residence behind Fort Mackinac. Two years later he was replaced by Samuel D. Poole. Their responsibilities were nearly the same as the post commandant except that they had no soldiers to help with park chores.

The superintendent and commission were responsive to the needs of the cottagers and island citizens. In 1896 several cottagers signed a petition asking that the island's historic spots, andespecially the area around the fort, be exempt from improvement or leasing. The commission passed a resolution endorsing their requests.[33] The following year, a committee was appointed to plat and partition the old fort garden and set rental prices for the lots. The garden was situated below the fort on the island's main street. When application was made to lease the property west of the public schoolhouse for a hotel site, the cottagers again voiced their

Above: Anne Cottage *was originally constructed for Alvin Hert in 1899. This was one of three cottages constructed on property leased from Mackinac Island State Park Commission east of the old fort garden (now Marquette Park).*

Below: Anne Cottage, *enlarged and remodeled in the early 20th century, features the strong horizontal lines, broad hipped roof and widely overhanging eaves typical of Prairie Style architecture.*

Packard cottage at British Landing.

dissatisfaction. The application was denied and the commission voted to dedicate the area to "monumental and ornamental purposes."[34]

In 1898 the commission hired Byron E. Cubley to survey the land on the east side of the old fort garden and divide it into three building lots. By 1901 all three lots had been leased, and summer cottages were erected on lots one and three. In 1899 George T. Arnold built a year-round residence on lot two. From his wide veranda Arnold could conveniently keep watch on his dock across the bay where the Arnold Line Steamers were moored.

In 1896 the commission began construction of the shore boulevard and by the turn of the century there was a fine graveled road around the entire island. The new road allowed access to a large piece of private property known as the Early farm on the northeast side of the island. A few individuals interested in building summer cottages along the shore near British Lansing purchased parcels of land from the Early family. Among the new cottagers at British Lansing were George and Caroline Packard. In 1903 Packard hired contractor G.W. Dewey and his son to build

his cottage, which had been designed by Henry Barker, an architect and old friend of Packard's from Providence, Rhode Island.

The new park administration assisted cottagers who were trying to sell or lease their homes. In several cases Samuel Poole acted as an intermediary, uniting sellers and prospective buyers. He even extended his services to Annex cottagers. In April of 1900 P. J. Cunningham contacted the superintendent about securing a cottage for the coming summer. Poole suggested a cottage on the East Bluff. However, when Cunningham replied seeking information about the Douglass cottage in the Annex, the superintendent provided a thorough description, his estimate of the value and his personal opinion that it was in a desirable location.[35]

Cottage construction slowed after the park was transferred from federal to state authorities. Besides those at British Landing and in the village, only four cottages were built between 1895 and 1917, two in the Annex and two on the East Bluff. This lag was not caused by the change in administration, but because most of the desirable lots were already occupied.

CHAPTER FOUR
Summer Cottage Life

"But, while Mackinac generally gets its full credit
for natural beauty and healthy atmosphere,
one of its main advantages — and one that comes first
in the list of requirements at the Eastern resorts —
is left entirely out of consideration — its cottage life."

- Petoskey Daily Resorter, August 13, 1891

When cottagers came to Mackinac Island they were on vacation. For two months they were free from the demands of their jobs, their hometown social obligations and the humdrum of everyday life.

Most cottagers wanted a relaxed and informal resort experience during the summer. While they enjoyed the island's rustic northern woods environment most cottagers made sure to bring along luxuries to accommodate their affluent lifestyle.

After the Eating House was closed, the Annex residents joined other cottagers in preparing their own meals or in eating in one of the island hotels. They outfitted their kitchens with cook stoves and filled their cupboards with pots and pans. Dining room sideboards were liberally stocked with silverware and fine china. The lady of the house often purchased the groceries and determined the bill of fare. As a cook for Colonel and Mrs. Henry Davis, Agnes Shine recalled that shopping was a social event for the cottage ladies:

> *There were so many of those ladies, real refined women, and they used to walk downtown with their hats and gloves on. They would go to the post office and down to the grocery store and to the meat market.*

Then they would have their chats, and their coachmen would come after them.[1]

Cottagers were concerned about getting and keeping fresh food during the summer. Many purchased whitefish and lake trout from local fishermen and fresh meat from Hoban's or Donnelly's meat market. Perishables were kept in ice boxes cooled by blocks of ice which island residents cut during the previous winter. The ice, delivered by horse and dray, was sometimes stored in an ice house behind the cottage. Some of the more industrious summer residents planted vegetable gardens and kept cows and chickens. The cows were especially valuable as they provided fresh milk for children and other dairy products. But not everyone liked the idea of having cows wandering around the cottage communities. In 1885 Illinois congressman William Springer wrote:

> *We would be glad to spend our summers at Mackinac, but our experience last season has somewhat discouraged us. Owing to the 'cow bell nuisance' Mrs. Springer did not get the rest desired and in consequence failed to improve in health at all - and as a result has been ill the entire winter.[2]*

Water supply also was an important consideration. Many early residents had their drinking water delivered by Mike Nawacigick, a Native American drayman who drew the water from the spring below Fort Mackinac near Trinity Church. Cottagers relied on rain water gathered by a system of eaves troughs and barrels for bathing and washing. Dissatisfied with these arrangements, many cottagers devised ingenious schemes for drawing cool, fresh water directly out of the surrounding waters. In 1886 William Westover improvised a system of wires, pails and a windlass to bring water from the Straits of Mackinac up the steep cliff to his West Bluff cottage.[3] Frank Clark and David Hogg

Opposite page: Family and friends gather for a festive celebration at the Walter C. Newberry cottage on the West Bluff.

Above top: Daisy Number 6 was rented for a summer from a Cheboygan farmer by Annex cottager Luther Day. (Mrs. Clemens Gunn)

Bottom: Downspout and water barrel on H.L. Jenness' East Bluff cottage.

Above: Domestic servants employed by the Sheley family at Cedar Point cottage.

Below: Daisy Blodgett (third from right) and her daughter Helen (second from right) host a group of friends at a swimming party in front of their West Bluff cottage, 1913. (Hope Goodwin)

installed more technologically advanced systems featuring motorized pumps which drew lake water up the bluff to their cottages.[4] East Bluff cottagers did not enjoy direct access to the lake and so John Owen and C. C. Bowen paid Gregg Lambert $15 a year for the right to set a pump house on his lakeside property on the east end of the village.[5] Water was drawn from the harbor and pumped through a system of pipes to holding tanks at each of their cottages. When Henry Petersen moved into his new cottage on the top of the East Bluff in 1899, he asked the park commission to run pipes from its water supply in the fort to the East Bluff. Superintendent Poole agreed to provide the water if the cottagers would lay the pipes, or pay the park to do the work. They eagerly agreed, and eleven cottagers were connected to the park's water system by the following year.[6] These individual water systems were replaced in 1901 when the island community installed a modern municipal water works.

Diving platform in front of West Bluff cottages, 1913. (Hope Goodwin)

Many cottagers brought servants who took care of the domestic chores. Cooks prepared the daily meals for the family and other servants. They also cooked for dinner parties and luncheons, which were common social events. Maids polished furniture, swept the floors, made the beds and cared for the special needs of any house guests. Nurses fed, bathed and cared for the children. Male servants cut firewood, hauled ice to the refrigerator, milked the cows and occasionally acted as butlers. The servants were usually supervised by the lady of the house because her husband often traveled home to attend to his work. Concerned about leaving their wives and children alone, Ernst Puttkammer and L. L. McArthur installed a dry cell telephone between their neighboring cottages. Although the phone was designed for emergencies, it was more often used for friendly conversations.[7]

A staff of servants provided leisure time for the cottager. With the concerns of his household left in able hands, the summer resident turned his attention to the social activities of the island.

By the 1890s the island was known as a fashionable place for those who wanted to "kick up their heels." Angeline Teal described the island's social life by comparing it to the neighboring resort town of Petoskey:

> *Mackinac is well supplied with spacious and elegant hotels, filled during the season with summer tourists. They dance a great deal there. At Petoskey it is different. The near proximity of several resorts which are under the control of religious associations, and the character of the multitudes who flock to these resorts during the camp-meeting season, has left its imprint on the entire social life of the place. He who, in the language of a gay worldling of my acquaintance, likes 'a very little Sunday-school and a good deal of hop' in his summer's recreations, will naturally prefer Mackinac.[8]*

The Grand Hotel orchestra provided afternoon entertainment on the hotel's spacious front porch.

Entertaining within the cottage was an important part of summer social life. Certain cottagers took great delight in using their homes for social gatherings. Delos and Daisy Blodgett always brought a force of servants, horses, carriages and other conveniences designed to entertain their friends royally. Their daughter, Helen Erwin, explained the type of evening entertainment which might follow a dinner party:

> *…the guests would often gather around a large open fireplace…a large basket stood before the fire and in it were small bundles of wood, perhaps not more than a foot or two long and a few inches wide. These pieces of wood were tied into bundles with pieces of string or narrow ribbon. Each person was given, in turn, a faggot (as they were called) to toss on the fire and while the wood burned this person was supposed to tell a short story or incident that lasted until the wood was consumed.*[9]

Mrs. Blodgett enjoyed parties which stimulated good conversation. On the evening of August 12, 1894 she invited about thirty friends to her cottage to compete in a ghost story telling contest. For their blood-curdling tales Allyne Stocking won the ladies' prize, and John Batten carried away the gentlemen's honors.

The Annex Eating House was the scene of many festive gatherings. On August 22, 1883 Gurdon Hubbard was joined by friends and neighbors in the building's reception and dining rooms, where they celebrated his eighty-first birthday. Officers from the fort attended and the military band provided the music. Judge H. G. Wells honored Hubbard by recounting his early days as a fur trader on Mackinac Island.[10]

The island's hotels provided much of the social activity for the cottagers. Summer residents turned out *en masse* for the weekly dances. During the summer of 1896 the Island House hotel held its "hops" on Mondays and Wednesdays, and its formal dances on Fridays.[11] The Grand Hotel ballroom was the scene of the most elegant and fashionable dances. The hardwood floor was surrounded by decorative wooden railings and box seats. Spectators often gathered in the balcony above the dance floor. The gentlemen always dressed in "white tie and tails" and the ladies wore their finest ball gowns and trains.[12] In the early 1890s cottagers danced into the early morning to the music of Len H. Salisbury's orchestra.

Energized by the island's refreshing environment and festive atmosphere, cottagers participated in sporting events and other outdoor activities. Mackinac roads and trails provided a beautiful setting for horseback riding and driving. Most of the equestrienne cottagers brought their own horses and carriages from home, and kept them in their own stables. Maintaining a full stable was a time-consuming job. Coachmen and grooms were often added to the staff and acted as drivers, cleaned stalls, oiled the tack and prepared horse and rider for the daily jaunt.

Those who wanted to avoid this bother could rent a horse and buggy from the Grand Hotel stables or Starr's Livery. G. W. Dickenson maintained a small stable in the Annex while managing the Eating House. He made his rigs available to both cottagers and the general public.[13]

For a change of pace, cottagers occasionally took excursions to neighboring towns and resorts. The steam-powered ferry boats *Charles West*, *Algomah* and *Islander* frequently journeyed to Les Cheneaux Islands, Cheboygan, St. Ignace and Mackinaw City. This gave the island crowd

Top: The Blodgett family pony cart with nanny and small children in 1895.

Bottom: Same pony cart several years later with grown children and a new "horse." (Hope Goodwin)

a chance to do some shopping, sightseeing and visiting. Most excursions were day trips, but cottagers also went on extended hunting and fishing expeditions. During August of 1887, Bishop Harris closed his Annex home for a few days while he went trout fishing on Lake Superior.[14]

Several cottagers owned steam yachts and sailboats which they moored in the island's bay during the summer. They used their boats for fishing trips, excursions, racing and entertaining.

Many of the vessels, such as John Cudahy's *Gerald C.*, were seventy feet or longer, providing ample room for parties and informal gatherings. Decks were lavishly decorated with oriental rugs and wicker chairs and canvas tarps which kept the pale-skinned Victorians out of the sunlight.

Michael Cudahy used his steam yacht *Catherine C.* to go to church every Sunday morning. The boat, docked below his Annex cottage, was used to transport the family to Ste. Anne's Catholic Church in town.[15] The crews needed to operate and maintain vessels of this size usually sailed the boat north to the island early in the summer and returned it to home port in the fall, while the owners rode in the more comfortable accommodations of large commercial passenger boats.

Tennis and golf were both available to Mackinac Island summer cottagers in the 1890s. Several tennis courts were available for the racquet crowd. Mission House, with a court on its front lawn, and the Grand Hotel, featuring "two of the best clay courts in northern Michigan," tried to lure guests by offering tennis. Annex cottagers had a short-lived tennis court on the commons and private courts were constructed on the West Bluff and at Stonecliffe. In 1905 a number of East Bluff cottagers petitioned the Mackinac Island State Park Commission for a piece of land behind the

Above: Tennis courts on the grounds in front of the Grand Hotel.

Left: The well-appointed deck of a Mackinac yacht.

fort for a lawn tennis court. The request was approved, but the court was never built. While tennis received a lukewarm reception, golf became the rage among the summer crowd.

In the 1890s four Annex physicians, Drs. McArthur, Billings, McKenna, and Patrick, and West Bluff cottager William Amberg, formed the Mackinac Island Golf Club and laid out a small five-hole golf course in a meadow beyond the Annex.[16] The twenty-five acre plot was owned by H. C. Gray who offered to sell the property to the golf club in the fall of 1897.[17] Preferring a larger tract of land on which they could establish a full-size course, the club declined Gray's offer and made arrangements to lease and develop a portion of Peter Early's farm which was the site of the 1814 Battle of Mackinac Island.

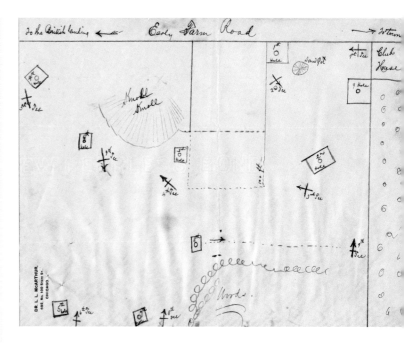

The new course was designed and staked in October 1898 by Alex Smith, a Scottish-born golf professional. Island contractor Frank Rounds received the contract to build the course which was completed in August 1899. Club members named the new course *Wawashkamo*, an Ojibway name meaning "Crooked Trail" which was, perhaps, a humorous reference to the path taken by amateur golfers following their shots down the fairway.

Men's and women's handicap tournaments were held at Wawashkamo during the following summer. Thomas O'Brien won the gentlemen's contest and received two dozen golf balls for his victory. Eight women participated in the ladies tournament. The winner was Miss Brittain, whose score of fifty-four bested Mrs. McArthur by one stroke.[18]

The highlight of the summer's sporting events in the 1890s was the annual field-day sponsored by Grand Hotel. The hotel's social director organized the activities which were open to all island visitors and residents. The events included a bell-hops' wash tub race, a dog swimming race, a gentlemen's swimming contest, horse races and a rugby football match. A five dollar prize was awarded to the person who could reach the end of a twenty-five-foot greased pole extending over the water from a dock below Grand Hotel.[19] In 1896 the field-day began with a yacht race, boasting five entries in the first class category. West Bluff cottager Frank Hecker won the race on board *Samoa*. His prize, appropriately enough, was a Grand Hotel flag.[20]

Summer life was a delightful change of pace for the island cottagers. They perceived of their island experiences as an intriguing combination of rustic backwoods living and fashionable resort life, a rejuvenating break from their usual routines. Stimulated by the refreshing environment, they soon forgot the cares of the world and indulged themselves in the daily activities of their island refuge.

CHAPTER FIVE

The Architecture of the Summer Cottages

"Handsome and elegant cottages are the only kind
on Mackinac Island. They are the best in architecture
and the richest in furnishings that wealth can recommend."

- Petoskey Daily Reporter, April 24, 1893

The summer cottages on Mackinac Island reflect a variety of late nineteenth and early twentieth century architectural styles which fall into two broad categories.

The earlier cottages are small and modest. They employ simple plans and restrained ornamentation, and their designs come from pattern books or the imagination of local builders. The later cottages are larger and more decorative. These homes were usually designed by trained architects and they more closely resemble traditional architectural styles.

The final appearance of all the island cottages was determined, in part, by factors other than imagination or style. Since the cottages were used only in the summer, they did not have to be insulated and the exterior walls of the less formal rooms were left unsheathed. The exposed studs were often trimmed with a decorative bead and finished with a natural stain. Coal burning furnaces were installed in some of the homes, but central heating systems were usually unnecessary. Rooms were large and airy with an abundance of windows and doors. Interiors were designed for the flow of fresh air, rather than for the containment of heat. Similarly, cottages were generously supplied with open porches, verandas and belvederes. These elements were designed to integrate the pleasant summer environment with the interior of the cottage.

Cottage designers also needed to provide living quarters for servants.

In some cases there was ample room on the third floor or in the attic. Occasionally, kitchens and pantries were located in separate buildings which were attached to the cottage by a hall or breezeway. The second floor of these additions was set aside for servant quarters. Barns were usually made large enough to accommodate stablemen and grooms in second floor apartments.

Floor plans were arranged so that the cottage was conducive to entertaining. Large living rooms and porches dominated the front of most cottages. They were connected by sets of double doors and were designed to flow together and suggest openness. This was the entertainment center of the cottage.

The availability and transportation of materials also determined the buildings' appearance. All building supplies had to be brought to the island from the mainland. Indigenous limestone was occasionally used for foundations and retaining walls, but it was impractical for major construction. Wood was the favored construction material. It was abundant and cheap in northern Michigan and it was more easily transported than stone or brick. Furthermore, frame houses could be built fast enough to keep up with the construction boom.

Craig Mawr *cottage on the East Bluff.*

The Vernacular Carpenter Gothic Cottages

The early Mackinac Island cottages were small and inexpensive and reflected the modest nature of the cottage communities in the early 1880s.

Cottagers chose styles from popular architectural pattern books or relied on the time-tested designs of the cottage builders. The ornamentation was light and simple, based on Gothic Revival patterns as they were interpreted by the local carpenter.

Above: The William Gilbert cottage (1889), West Bluff. Many of the early island cottages were built by Charles W. Caskey and are easily identified by their design. The Gilbert cottage floor plan (right) is a typical Caskey design. Its large three-sided porch forms a "U" around the front wing of the cottage. Within the "U" is a single bay containing a sitting room on the first floor. The dining room and a bedroom are behind the sitting room in another single bay which runs perendicular to the front wing. The kitchen, pantry, and servant's quarters are in a single story lean-to attached to the back of the cottage. There are three bedrooms on the second floor.

Opposite top: Built in 1882, the Alanson Sheley cottage Small Point, *with its steep pitched roofs and dormers trimmed with decoratively cut "gingerbread" ornamentation, is Mackinac's best excellent example of Gothic Revival architecture.*

Opposite bottom: The interior of an early, vernacular Mackinac Island cottage decorated in typical Victorian style. An 1886 Cheboygan Democrat *article reported, "Some of the interiors of the cottages are delightful. The general character of the parlors are the same. A profusion of rugs, rattan and wicker chairs of all shapes, sizes and colors, cushioned with mossy plush, and an assortment of bric-a-brac and etchings tastefully arranged around the rooms."*

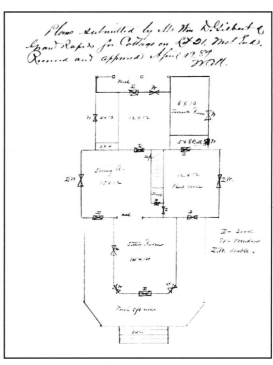

Opposite page: Episcopal Diocese of Michigan cottage (1885), Hubbard's Annex. The exterior of Caskey's cottages are very similar. Most have gabled roofs, railed porches, interior chimneys and horizontal siding. The wooden trim consists of sawn ornaments applied to the gables, eaves and porches.

Below: William McCourtie Cottage (1883), Hubbard's Annex. Charles Caskey's cottages are similar to the thousands of symmetrical, cross-gabled houses that were built throughout the United States between 1850 and 1900. Each cottage was made distinct by its paint color, style of trim, porch railing, window placement and location of the front steps. (Clarke Historical Library, Central Michigan University)

The L.L. McArthur cottage (1885), Hubbard's Annex. This cottage has a typical Caskey floor plan, but a bracketed second story porch and pierced eave trim in the front gable give it a unique Swiss Chalet appearance. The gabled overhanging roof that extends from the porch over the front steps also sets this cottage apart from others built by Caskey.

*Below: Charles Caskey cottage (1884), Hubbard's Annex.
Interestingly enough, when Caskey built his own cottage, he
abandoned his usual plan for one that was considerably larger
and more elaborate. The south facade contained two large
gables decorated with the same style vergeboards and trim.
A square tower rose between the two gables and was topped
by a concave tent roof with a small dormer window on
each side. The cottage's clapboard and shingle siding was
decorated with an overlay of horizontal and vertical boards
that were purely decorative and symbolized the unseen
structural members. This was typical of the architectural
style since named 'Stick Style'. The steeply pitched rooms,
projecting eaves and diagonal braces supporting the veranda
roof are all common elements of this style. (Lorna Strauss)*

The surge in growth which the cottage communities experienced in the late 1880s and 1890s coincided with the emerging popularity of Victorian Queen Anne architecture. Queen Anne homes became the defining style of the "Gilded Age."

Large, asymmetrical and picturesque, this style represented a break from the box-like, balanced gothic cottages built by the early island cottagers. Many of Mackinac's premier Queen Anne cottages were designed by architect Asbury W. Buckley. Buckley's wooden castles suggested variety and irregularity and a strong sense of vertical massing. This effect was achieved by the use of different wall surfaces and textures, sweeping verandas which dominated the main facade, a multitude of various shaped roofs and an endless array of polygonal towers, belvederes and other decorative elements.

Alexander Hannah's cottage Cairngorm (1892), West Bluff. The prime facade of a Queen Anne cottage was typically dominated by a long sweeping veranda connected to a large, open living hall inside. In later years, verandas were often remodeled to include a glassed-in sun porch. When not relaxing on his veranda (opposite top), Hannah could retreat into his lavishly decorated living hall (opposite bottom).

The William Amberg (opposite top), George T. Arnold (opposite bottom), and David Hogg (this page) cottages are excellent examples of Queen Anne architecture. Each incorporates the usual combination of protruding bays and towers and receding porches and verandas, contrasting shapes and forms, a variety of decoratively cut siding shingles and vertical massing.

John Cudahy's West Bluff cottage The Pines *(1888).*

Opposite top: Cudahy's style-setting cottage was the first Queen Anne constructed on the West Bluff. Within five years, four of his neighbors tore down their smaller vernacular style homes and built similar large, opulent Queen Anne homes.

Opposite bottom: The living hall of the Cudahy cottage as it appeared around 1900. The large brick fireplace and open stairway and landing are typical of the island's Queen Anne cottages.

A varnished natural wood finish was used throughout the house, including the second floor bedrooms (above) and the dining room (right).

Charles and Clifford Anthony built Windermere *on Biddle Point in 1887. The cottage, subsequently converted into a hotel of the same name, was designed by Richard Rickman of Peoria, Illinois. The cottage's most interesting feature is its lighthouse-style tower, a particularly appropriate design for lake or seaside cottages.*

Above: When remodeling Delos Blodgett's West Bluff cottage Casa Verano *in 1892, architect Asbury W. Buckley surrounded a massive gambrel roof with a variety of Queen Anne elements including a sweeping veranda, decoratively cut siding shingles and a variety of contrasting materials and shapes.*

Below: Casa Verano's *living hall was decorated with elegant wood trim, an appropriate touch for a lumber baron like Blodgett.*

The Shingle Style Cottages

The John Atkinson cottage was built in 1885 and remodeled to its Shingle Style appearance in 1890. The unity-in-design concept is achieved not only by the exclusive use of shingles, but also in the alternating scalloped and pointed openings which begin in the foundation and continue to the porch and octagonal tower. The front parlor, contained in the base of the tower, allows free and easy access to the surrounding porch.

Shingle Style cottage architecture was popular on Mackinac Island and in other resort towns, especially on the east coast.[2] Like Queen Anne cottages, they are typically large and asymmetrical and the facades are flexible enough to allow for open interiors and rambling porches. But here is where the similarities end. While Queen Anne cottages emphasize irregular vertical massing, Shingle Style cottages suggest horizontal flow and surface unity. The style is characterized by a uniform, thin coating of unpainted shingles on the exterior walls which allows the building's various pieces to blend together, creating a simple, monochromatic appearance.

This page: The H.L. Jenness cottage, 1892. The stained shingles on the Jenness cottage give it a rustic look that was characteristic of Shingle Style cottages. The roof sweeps down from the ridge to cover the veranda and then follows the gentle flow of the rounded porch roof. The eaves of the roof are close to the walls and are covered with shingles, preserving and emphasizing the building's homogenous appearance. Typically, the living hall is located inside the porch, and the two are joined by use of large windows and doors.

Opposite top: In 1891, E.P. Barnard hired Charles Caskey to build a simple cross-gabled vernacular cottage for him on the East Bluff. The following year, the cottage was completely remodeled and the facade took on a new, shingled appearance. Although the crossed gables of the Caskey cottage are still evident, the shingles and scalloped porch openings create a softer, more unified impression. The tower on the west side does not protrude, but gently blends with the rest of the building. The porches are contained within the shingled exterior, and are an integral part of the cottage's summer living area.

Opposite bottom: John Owen cottage, 1887. The location of the windows, strong eave line, long veranda, and even the tiny pointed shingles emphasize the horizontal flow of the Owen cottage. The corners are gently rounded and the cottage seems to be molded into a single unit without distracting protuberances or harsh edges.

The broad gambrel roof and four small casement windows of the Susan Blodgett Lowe cottage are typical shingle style features. Like shingle siding, the large intersecting roofs unite the volumes of the cottage.

In 1901, the Mackinac Island State Park Commission leased the West Fort lot to Lawrence Young. Young hired Chicago architect Frederick Perkins to design the cottage, which was built by island contractor Patrick Doud and a crew of 75 carpenters. The dark shingled siding and horizontal band of windows tucked neatly under the flared eaves are reminiscent of the Shingle Style. In 1945 the State of Michigan purchased the cottage for $15,000 and since that time it has served as the official summer residence of the state's governor.

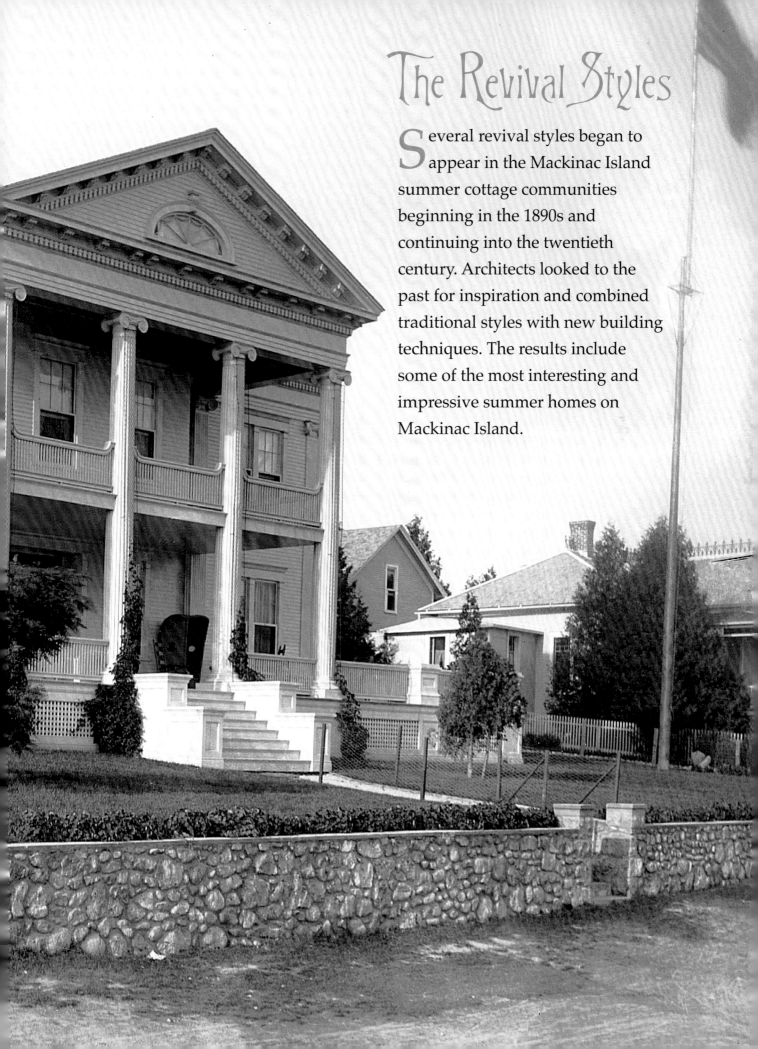

The Revival Styles

S everal revival styles began to appear in the Mackinac Island summer cottage communities beginning in the 1890s and continuing into the twentieth century. Architects looked to the past for inspiration and combined traditional styles with new building techniques. The results include some of the most interesting and impressive summer homes on Mackinac Island.

In 1900, Milton Tootle Jr., of St. Joseph, Missouri, purchased George Smith's East Bluff cottage and remodeled it in the Neo-Classical Revival style. The result is a symmetrical building with a large pediment roof over a two-tiered portico supported by Ionic columns. Also typical of this style are the narrow clapboards, flat, railed roof, Ionic pilaster corner boards and the rectangular transom over the front door.

Above: Entrance hall of the Milton Tootle, Jr. cottage, ca. 1905. Neo-Classical Revival style saw a return to symmetrical floor plans of earlier styles. The stairway is in the center of the large entracne hall, which is flanked by the living room to one side and the dining room to the other.

Below: The Milton Tootle, Jr. family in the garden behind his cottage.

In the late 1890s, Charles Bowen remodeled his East Bluff cottage in the Neo-Classical Revival style. He converted a simple Caskey-style cottage into an elaborate double house connected by a two-tier portico with Ionic columns running the entire length of the building.

The John Weiss cottage Lover's Leap (1905) in Hubbard's Annex is an excellent example of Colonial Revival architecture. It has a symmetrical, rectangular plan and a large gambrel roof with a Palladian window on either end. The large portico on the north elevation is supported by Ionic columns and is crowned with a pediment. The veranda on the south facade is divided in the middle by a two-tier portico in which Doric columns are used. This combination of orders reflects the type of inconsistency or historical inaccuracy that distinguishes Colonial Revival homes from their 18th century counterparts.

Above: In 1894 A.W. Buckley designed and built this $10,000 Colonial Revival cottage for Henry Davis of Springfield, Illinois. Typical of the style is the large hipped roof topped with a flat deck which is surrounded by an iron railing. Gable dormers with Palladian windows project from the east, west, and south slopes of the roof and are the focal point of the symmetrical facades. Below: The V.W. Mather cottage, constructed on the East Bluff in 1900, is a smaller version of Colonial Revival styling.

In 1897, Michael Cudahy sold his Hubbard's Annex cottage to his brother Edward and moved his summer residence to California. Not satisfied with life on the West Coast, he returned to Mackinac Island and constructed Stonecliffe on 150 acres of private property in 1904.

Above: The Cudahy family poses in front of Stonecliffe *in the winter during construction. (University of Illinois at Urbana-Champaign).*

Below: Stonecliffe *is an excellent example of English Revival architecture. Designed by Frederick Perkins, the steep pitched gabled roofs and dormers, leaded glass casement windows, ornate chimneys and half-timbered exterior walls with stucco siding are typical of this post-Victorian style.*

Above: A large, baronial fireplace is the focal point of the Stonecliffe *living room. Below: The* Stonecliffe *entrance hall is trimmed with handsome dark wood paneling. (University of Illinois at Urbana-Champaign)*

In 1917, Selim McArthur hired Patrick Doud to construct this cottage in Hubbard's Annex. The one story cottage has a low-pitched, hipped roof with exterior chimneys on either end. The large, eight-light casement windows form a horizontal band around the structure and emphasize its low profile. It falls into the broad category of Bungalow style. The McArthur cottage represents a break from picturesque Victorian and Revival Style cottages and a step towards the simplicity of ranch style architecture which became popular later in the 20th century.

Map Index to Cottages & Owners

The maps of the East Bluff, West Bluff, and Hubbard's Annex show the development of cottages in each area. The date of construction for each cottage is shown within the representative box. If an earlier cottage once occupied that site, its date of construction is shown in parentheses. Cottages that have been torn down, or burned down, and not replaced, are indicated by a broken-line box. For cottages on the East and West Bluffs the lot number is adjacent to the particular box. On the Hubbard's Annex map both lot and block numbers are given. Unless otherwise indicated, the lot number is shown on the left side of the slash and the block number on the right.

Following is a list of the first owners of the cottages. If the cottage has been replaced or substantially remodeled, the owner's name at that time is also given. If the builder or architect is known, their name is also provided.

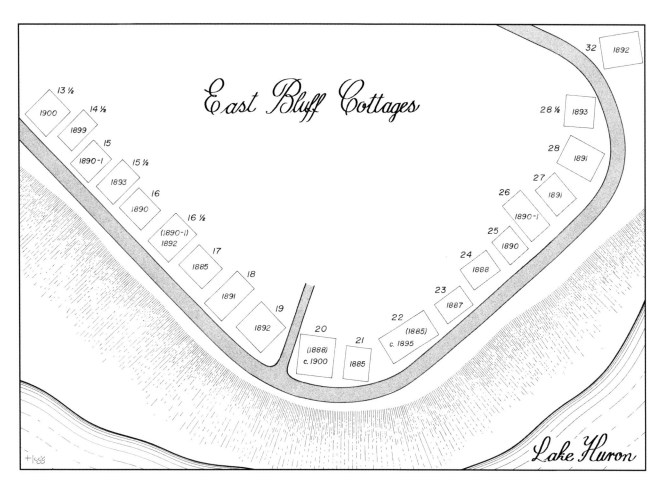

East Bluff Cottages

Lake Huron

Lot#	Owner/Builder
13 1/2	V.W. Mather, 1900 Frank Rounds, builder
14 1/2	Henry F. Peterson, 1899
15	Henry Freeman, 1890-1 Matt Elliott, builder
15 1/2	Elstner Fisher, 1893 G.W. Catell, builder
16	Meade C. Williams, 1890
16 1/2	E.P. Barnard, 1890-1 Remodeled, 1892
17	John Atkinson, 1885 A.G. Couchois, builder Remodeled, ca. 1890
18	T.F. Spangler, 1891 Matt Elliott, builder
19	H.L. Jenness, 1892 Matt Elliott, builder

Lot#	Owner/Builder
20	G.W. Smith, 1888 W.L.B. Jenney, Architect C.W. Caskey, builder Milton Tootle, ca. 1900 Patrick Doud, builder
21	Phoebe Gehr, 1885 C.W. Caskey, builder
22	Charlotte Warren, 1885 C.W. Caskey, builder C. C. Bowen, ca. 1895
23	Jane Owen, 1887
24	Montgomery Hamilton, 1888
25	G.E. Bursley, 1890
26	Mrs. James Walsh, 1890-1
27	Anne Morrison, 1891
28	R.S. Taylor, 1891 Matt Elliott, builder
28 1/2	Stephan Bond, 1893
32	John Batten, 1892 Matt Elliott, builder

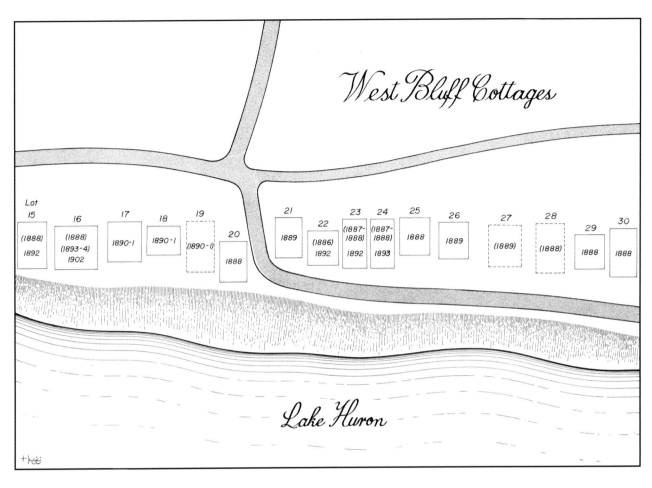

Lot #	Owner/Builder/Architect
15	Frank Clark, 1888 Edwin Zander, builder Delos Blodgett, 1892 A.W. Buckley, architect
16	George Stockbridge, 1888 Edwin Zander, builder Edwin Pitkin, 1893-94 A.W. Buckley, architect H.H. Hanna, 1902 A.W. Buckley, architect
17	Thomas A. White, 1890-91 A.W. Buckley, architect
18	John A. Edget, 1890-91
19	M.H. Lane, 1890-91 A.W. Buckley, architect (torn down)
20	Henry Leman, 1888
21	William D. Gilbert, 1889 C.W. Caskey, builder

Lot#	Owner/Builder/Architect
22	William Westover, 1886 William Amberg, 1892 A.W. Buckley, architect
23	Alexander Hannah, 1887-88 Remodeled, 1892 A.W. Buckley, architect
24	David Hogg, 1887-8 Remodeled, 1893 A.W. Buckley, architect
25	John Cudahy, 1888
26	Delos Blodgett, 1889
27	E. Crofton Fox, 1889 (torn down)
28	William O. Hughart, 1888 (burned to the ground, December 14, 1978)
29	Thomas J. O'Brien, 1888
30	Walter C. Newberry, 1888

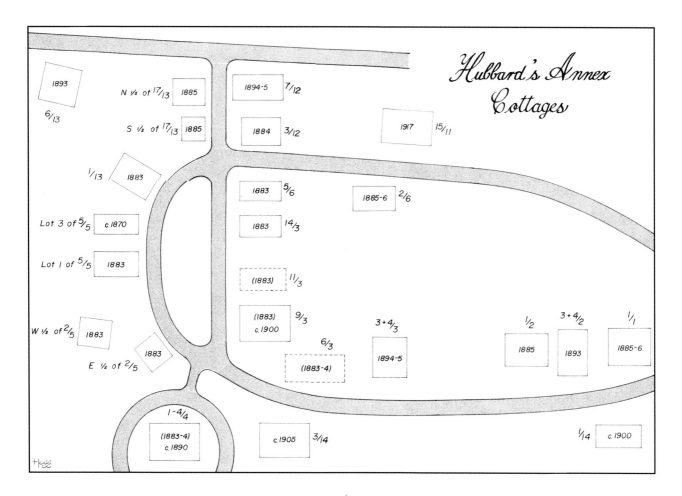

Hubbard's Annex Cottages

Lot #, Block #	Owner/Builder/Architect
1, 1	Hugh McCurdy, 1885-86
1, 2 1885	Episcopal Diocese of Michigan, C.W. Caskey, builder
3 & 4, 2	H.W. Longyear, S.T. Douglas, 1893 C.W. Caskey, builder
3 & 4, 3	Henry Davis, 1894-5 A.W. Buckley, architect and builder
6, 3	E.F. Sweet, 1883-84 (torn down)
9, 3	Frank Clark, 1883 Remodeled, ca. 1900
11, 3	"Eating House," 1883 (torn down)
14, 3	Theodore P. Shelton, 1883 C.W. Caskey, builder
All of Block 4	Francis Stockbridge, 1883-84 Michael Cudahy, c. 1890
W 1/2 of L2, B5	Hezekiah Wells, 1883 C.W. Caskey, builder
E 1/2 of L2, B5	William H. McCourtie, 1883 C.W. Caskey, builder
L1 of L5, B5	Gurdon Hubbard, 1883 C.W. Caskey, builder

Lot #, Block #	Owner/Builder/Architect
L3 of L5, B5	Gurdon Hubbard, c. 1870
2, 6	Gurdon Hubbard, 1885-86 William Dunning, 1888
5, 6	D.C. Holliday, 1883 C.W. Caskey, builder
15, 11	Selim McArthur, 1917 Patrick Doud, builder
3, 12	C.W. Caskey, 1884 C.W. Caskey, builder
7, 12	Ernst Puttkammer, 1894-95
1, 13	Otis W. Johnson, 1883 C.W. Caskey, builder
6, 13	A.D. Silverhorn, 1893
N 1/2 of L17, B13	John Belden, 1885 C.W. Caskey, builder
S 1/2 of L17, B13	Dr. L.L. McArthur, 1885 C.W. Caskey, builder
1, 14	ca.1900 (as gazebo) ca. 1935 converted to cottage, W.S. Woodfill
3, 14	John Weiss, ca. 1905 Patrick Doud, builder

NOTES

Chapter 1. Development of Mackinac Island as a Summer Resort

[1] Henry Schoolcraft, *Summary Narrative of an Exploratory Expedition to the Sources of the Mississippi River in 1820*, quoted in Edwin O. Wood, *Historic Mackinac*, 2 vols. (New York: The MacMillan Co., 1918) 2:138.

[2] William Cullen Bryant, *Letters of a Traveller*, 1846, quoted in Edwin O. Wood, *Historic Mackinac*, 2 vols. (New York: The MacMillan Co., 1918) 2:379.

[3] Rev. J. A. Van Fleet, *Old and New Mackinac* (Ann Arbor: Courier Steam Printing House, 1870) 156.

[4] J. Disturnell, *The Great Lakes, or Inland Seas of America* (New York: Charles Scribner, 1863) 169.

[5] Charles Truscott, "Mackinac Island and the Passenger Boat Era." Mackinac State Historic Parks Library.

[6] Francis Duncan, "The History of the Detroit and Cleveland Steam Navigation Company: 1850-1951" (Ph.D., University of Chicago, 1954) 57-58.

[7] "The Reminiscences of Ernst Wilfred Puttkammer" Interview with Thomas Pfeiffelmann, 1973, Mackinac State Historic Parks Library, 9.

[8] James G. Inglis, *Northern Michigan: Handbook for Travellers* (1898; reprint, Grand Rapids: Black Letter Press, 1977) 52.

[9] J. Disturnell, *Island of Mackinac and its Vicinity* (1875; reprint, Cheboygan, Mich.: C.W. Page, 1977) 84.

[10] General Order No. 73, 27 July 1876, Records of the Judge Advocate General's Office, Military Reservation Division, 1809-1942, Reservation File, Mackinac National Park Section, Record Group 153, National Archives, Washington, D.C. (hereafter cited as RJAG).

[11] Ibid.

[12] James B. Fry to A.L. Hough, 2 September 1876, Records of the United States Army Continental Commands, Mackinac National Park, Record Group 393, National Archives, Washington, D.C. (hereafter cited RUSC) Letters sent 1875-1895.

Chapter 2. Origins of the Cottage Communities

[1] Lucius Geary to David Greene, 28 July 1835, Correspondence of the American Board of Commissioners for Foreign Missions, 18:6.1, V.1, No. 68, Houghton Library, Harvard University.

[2] W.B. Ogden to Charles Larnard, 8 August 1849, Records of the Quartermaster General, Consolidated Correspondence File on Fort Mackinac, 1819-1890, Record Group 92, National Archives, Washington, D.C.

[3] *Cheboygan Democrat*, 10 August 1882.

[4] Henry Hamilton, *Gurdon Saltonstall Hubbard: 1802-1886* (Chicago: Rand, McNally Co., 1888) 170-171.

[5] *The Autobiography of Gurdon Saltonstall Hubbard*, With an introduction by Caroline M. McIlvaine (Chicago: R. R. Donnelley and Sons Co., 1911) xiv-xxv.

[6] Francis Stockbridge to A. L. Hough, 15 November 1875 and O. W. Johnson to A. L. Hough, 13 November 1875, RUSC, Letters sent 1875-1895.

[7] A. L. Hough to Assistant Adjutant General, Military Division of the Atlantic, 24 November 1875, RUSC, Letters sent 1875-1895.

[8] Robert T. Lincoln to Thomas Ferry. 28 September 1882, RUSC, Letters sent 1875-1895.

[9] Ibid.

[10] William Springer to Robert T. Lincoln, 14 August 1884, RJAG, Box 27 A, Folder 2.

[11] George Brady to Robert T. Lincoln, 29 August 1884, RJAG, Box 27A, Folder 2.

[12] R. C. Drum to Commanding General, Department of the East, 30 October 1884, RJAG, Box 27 A, Folder 2.

[13] All of the steps in the administration of the park leases are mentioned frequently in RUSC, Letters sent 1875-1895.

[14] The necessary minimum cost of cottage construction is often mentioned in RUSC, Letters sent 1875-1895.

[15] G. Goodale to His Honor, The Mayor of Chicago, 26 July 1887, RUSC, Letters sent 1875-1895.

[16] Ibid.

[17] J. D. Bingham to E. M. Coates, 17 June 1891, RUSC, Letters sent 1875-1895.

Chapter 3. Establishment and Growth of the Cottage Communities

[1] *Cheboygan Democrat*, 8 July 1886; *Harbor Springs Northern Independent*, 8 September 1885.

[2] *Harbor Springs Northern Independent,* 8 September 1885.

[3] Helen Erwin to F. G. Hammitt, n.d., Bentley Historical Library, Ann Arbor, Michigan.

[4] Mrs. Ruth Sater to Phil Porter, 29 November 1979.

[5] *Harbor Springs Northern Independent*, 8 May 1882.

[6] Tax Assessment Rolls, Township of Holmes, Mackinac County, Michigan 1884, 1886-1891, Mackinac County Courthouse, St. Ignace, Michigan.

[7] *St. Ignace News*, 17 May 1887.

[8] Mrs. Ruth Sater to Phil Porter, 29 November 1979.

[9] Information on the changing ownership of the Annex cottages was found in the Tax Assessment Rolls, Township of Holmes, Mackinac County, Michigan, 1884, 1886-1891.

[10] E. W. Puttkammer, Interview by author, Mackinac Island, Michigan, June 1975.

[11] Phoebe Gehr to George Brady, 15 March 1885; C. Stewart Warren to George Brady, 7 April 1885, RUSC, Letters received and misc. papers, 1885-1895.

[12] *Harbor Springs Northern Independent*, 1 September 1885.

[13] *Petoskey Daily Resorter*, 13 August 1891.

[14] G. A. Goodale to Quartermaster General, Washington, D.C., 14 December 1887, RUSC, Letters sent 1875-1895.

[15] G. A. Goodale to Hon. Secretary of War, 31 December 1887, RUSC, Letters sent 1875-1895.

[16] *St. Ignace News*, 23 August 1887.

[17] George Stockbridge to G. A. Goodale, 20 June 1888, RUSC, Letters received and misc. papers, 1885-1895.

[18] *Petoskey Daily Resorter*, 26 August 1893.

[19] William Manning to Quartermaster General, Washington, D.C., 2 November 1887, RUSC, Letters sent 1875-1895.

[20] G. A. Goodale to Quartermaster General, Washington, D.C., 10 September 1889, RUSC, Letters sent 1875-1895.

[21] E. M. Coates to E. H. Pitkin, 29 November 1893, RUSC, Letters sent 1875-1895.

[22] E. M. Coates to Hon. Secretary of War, 31 December 1890, RUSC, Letters sent 1875-1895.

[23] G. A. Goodale to Quartermaster General, Washington, D.C., 23 April 1888, and E. M. Coates to Secretary of War, 31 December 1892, RUSC, Letters sent 1875-1895.

[24] G. K. Brady to Cashier, Detroit National Bank, 1 April 1885, RUSC, Letters sent 1875-1895.

[25] G. K. Brady to Secretary of War, 31 December 1885, RUSC, Letters sent 1875-1895.

[26] The disbursement of park funds is mentioned in the superintendent's annual reports to the secretary of war, found in RUSC, Letters sent 1875-1895.

[27] Quartermaster General to G. A. Goodale, 17 April 1888, RUSC, Letters received and misc. papers, 1885-1895.

[28] Richard Hulbert Diary, 1887-1891, October 1891, 188.

[29] Information on A. W. Buckley found in *Petoskey Daily Resorter*, 9 August 1894, 24 August 1894, 5 August 1901.

[30] Report of the Secretary of War, 26 November 1894, *Executive Documents of the House of Representatives, 53rd congress, 3rd session, 1894-95* (Washington: Government Printing Office. 1895) 31-32.

[31] Keith Widder, *Mackinac National Park, 1875-1895* (Lansing: Mackinac Island State Park Commission, 1975) 42-46.

[32] Mackinac Island State Park Commission (MISPC), *Minutes of Meetings*, 11 July 1895.

[33] MISPC, *Minutes of Meetings,* 12 August 1896.

[34] MISPC, *Minutes of Meetings,* 4 October 1899.

[35]Mackinac Island State Park Commission (MISPC), Correspondence of the Park Superintendent, 1896-1902, 28 April 1900, Mackinac State Historic Parks Archives

Chapter 4. Summer Cottage Life

[1] "The Reminiscences of Agnes Shine" (Agnes Shine interview by Thomas Pfeiffelmann, 1972. Transcribed by the Mackinac Island State Park Commission, Mackinac Island, Michigan, 1973) 3.

[2] William Springer to George K. Brady, 18 April 1885, RUSC, Letters received and misc. papers, 1885-1895.

[3] *Bay County Tribune,* 1886.

[4]E. W. Puttkammer, interview by author, Mackinac Island, Michigan, June 1975.

[5] George T. Arnold to Milton Tootle, Jr. 29 April 1898. Milton Tootle Correspondence, 1896-1897, Mackinac State Historic Parks Archives.

[6] MISPC, Correspondence of the Park Superintendent, 1896-1902, 22 May 1901.

[7] The Reminiscences of Ernst Wilfred Puttkammer" Interview with Thomas Pfeiffelmann, 1973, Mackinac State Historic Parks Archive, 5.

[8] Angeline Teal, "Petoskey and the Gem of the Straits," in *The Continent*, ed. Albion Tourgee, 36 (Philadelphia: Our Continent Publishing Co., 1883).

[9] Helen Erwin to F. G. Hammitt, n.d., Bentley Historical Library.

[10] *Cheboygan Democrat,* 6 September 1883.

[11] *St. Ignace News,* 18 July 1896.

[12] Helen Erwin to F. G. Hammitt, n.d., Bentley Historical Library.

[13] *Cheboygan Democrat,* 26 August 1886.

[14] *St. Ignace News,* 18 July 1887.

[15] E. W. Puttkammer, interview.

[16] E. W. Puttkammer, interview.

[17]H.C. Gray to Milton Tootle, 14 October 1897, Milton Tootle Correspondence, 1896-1897, Mackinac State Historic Parks Library.

[18]*Petoskey Daily Resorter,* 17 August 1900.

[19] *Petoskey Daily Resorter,* 29 August 1894.

[20] *Petoskey Daily Resorter,* 26 August 1896.

Chapter 5. The Architecture of the Summer Cottages

[1] The Stick Style was so named by Vincent Scully in *The Shingle Style and the Stick Style* (New Haven: Yale University Press, 1955).

[2]The Shingle Style was so named by Vincent Scully in *The Shingle Style and the Stick Style.*

BIBLIOGRAPHY

Primary Sources

LETTERS

Helen Erwin to Mrs. F. G. Hammit, "Notes sent on request to help her in writing seminar paper on 'Society Summer Sojourns' with reference to Mackinac Island, Michigan." n.d., Bentley Historical Library, Ann Arbor, Michigan.

Ruth Sater to Phil Porter, 29 November 1979. Author's private collection.

MUNICIPAL RECORDS

Village of Mackinac Island, Council Proceedings, 1875-1891, City Hall, Mackinac Island, Michigan.

Village of Mackinac Island, Ordinance Book, 1875-1899. City Hall, Mackinac Island, Michigan.

County of Mackinac, Holmes Township, Assessment Rolls, 1884, 1886-1892, 1895-1899,

NATIONAL ARCHIVES

Records of the Adjutant General's Office, Fort Mackinac, Michigan, Letters sent 1875-1886, Record Group 94, National Archives.

Records of the Judge Advocate General's Office, Military Reservation Division, 1809-1942, Reservation File, Mackinac National Park Section, Record Group 153, National Archives.

Records of the United States Army Continental Commands, Mackinac National Park, Record Group 393, National Archives.

NEWSPAPERS

Cheboygan (Mich.) *Democrat.* Weekly 1880-1927.

Cheboygan (Mich.) *News.* Weekly 1880-1913.

Emmet County (Mich.) *Independent.* Weekly 1878-1882.

Harbor Springs (Mich.) *Republican.* Weekly 1875-1925.

Northern Independent (Harbor Springs, Mich.) Weekly 1882-1887.

Petoskey (Mich.) *City Record.* Weekly 1878-1913.

Petoskey (Mich.) *Daily Resorter.* Daily 1883-1902.

Petoskey (Mich.) *Evening News.* Daily 1902-1953.

Petoskey (Mich.) *Independent.* Weekly 1905-1913.

Sault Ste. Marie (Mich.) *Democrat.* Weekly 1882-1887.

Sault Ste. Marie (Mich.) *News.* Weekly and Daily 1879-present.

St. Ignace (Mich.) *News.* Weekly and Semi-Weekly 1883-1900.

ORAL HISTORIES

"Reminiscences of Otto W. Lang," 1975, Mackinac State Historic Parks Library.

"Reminiscences of Wilfred Puttkammer," 1973, Mackinac State Historic Parks Library.

Puttkammer, Wilfred. June 1975. Interview by Phil Porter, transcription. Mackinac State Historic Parks Library.

"Reminiscences of Agnes Shine," 1972, Mackinac State Historic Parks Library.

PRINTED PRIMARY SOURCES

The Autobiography of Gurdon Saltonstall Hubbard, with introduction by Caroline M. McIlvaine. Chicago: R. R. Donnelley and Sons Company, 1911.

A Guide to the Health, Pleasure and Fishing Resorts of Northern Michigan, Reached by the Grand Rapids and Indiana Railroad. Published by the Passenger Department, W. O. Hughart President and General Manager, A. B. Leet, General Passenger Agent, 1879.

A Guide to the Health, Pleasure, Game and Fishing Resorts of Northern Michigan Reached by the Grand Rapids and Indiana Railroad. Published by the Passenger Department, 1882.

Disturnell, J. *The Great Lakes, or Inland Seas of America.* New York: Charles Scribner, Pub., 1863.

Early History of Michigan, with biographies of State Officers Members of Congress, Judges, and Legislators. Lansing: Thorp and Godfrey, State Printers and Binders, 1888.

Fisher, David and Frank Little, Editors. *Compendium of History and Biography of Kalamazoo County, Michigan.* Chicago: H. W. Bowan and Co., 1906.

Hamilton, Henry. *Gurdon Saltonstall Hubbard 1802-1886.* Collected from personal narrations and other sources, and arranged by his nephew, Henry Hamilton. Chicago: Rand, McNally Co., 1888.

Holly, Henry Hudson. *Holly's Country Seats*. New York: D. Appleton and Company, 1863.

Portrait and Biographical Record of Kalamazoo, Allegan and Van Buren Counties, Michigan. Chicago: Chapman Bros. 1892.

Richards, William C. "The Fairy Isle of Mackinac..." *Magazine of American History*, vol. XXVI, (1891): 22-35.

Teal, Angeline. "Petoskey and the Gem of the Straits" *The Continent*, vol. 3. No. 2, (1883).

Secondary Sources

Andrews, Wayne. *Architecture in Michigan, A Representative Photographic Survey*. Detroit: Wayne State University Press, 1967.

Bailey, John R. *Mackinac, Formerly Michilimackinac*. Grand Rapids: Tradesman Co., 1909.

Baxter, Albert. *History of the City of Grand Rapids*. New York: Munsell and Co., 1891.

Bicknell's Village Builder, A Victorian Architectural Guidebook. 1872. Reprint, with a new introduction and commentary by Paul Goeldner. Watkins Glen: The American Life Foundation, 1976.

Blumenson, John J. *Identifying American Architecture, A Pictorial guide to Styles and Terms, 1600-1945*. Nashville, Tenn.: American Association of State and Local History, 1977.

Brown, Arline M. *In the Wake of the Topinabee. Cherished Memories of Lakeside Cottagers*. Lancaster, Cal.: Hubbard Map Service, 1967.

Davidson, Marshall G. Ed. *The American Heritage History of Notable American Houses*. New York: American Heritage Publishing Co., 1971.

Downing, Andrew J. *The Architecture of Country Homes, including Designs for Cottages, Farm Houses, and Villas*. New York: D. Appleton and Co., 1850.

Downing, Andrew J. *Cottage Residences, Rural Architecture and Landscape Gardening*. 1842. Reprint with an introduction by Michael Hugo-Brunt. New York: Century House, 1967.

Durant, Samuel. *History of Kalamazoo County,*

Michigan. Philadelphia: Everts and Abbott, 1880.

Gill, Brendan and Dudley Witney. *Summer Places*. New York: Methuen, Inc., 1978.

Hogg, Victor. *A Survey of the Buildings of Mackinac Island*. Mackinac Island: Mackinac Island State Park Commission, 1971.

Maass, John. *The Gingerbread Age*. New York: Hawthorn Books, Inc., 1972.

Maass, John. *The Victorian Home in America*. New York: Hawthorn Books, Inc., 1972.

Men of Progress. Detroit: Evening News Association, 1900.

Petersen, Eugene T. *Mackinac Island, Its History in Pictures*, Mackinac Island: Mackinac Island State Park Commission, 1973.

Platt, Frederick *America's Gilded Age. Its Architecture and Decoration*. Cranbury, New Jersey: A. S. Barnes and Co., 1976.

Scully, Vincent J. *The Shingle Style and the Stick Style: Architectural Theory and Design from Richardson to the Origins of Wright*. New Haven: Yale University Press, 1971.

Sites, Susan and Lea Ann Sterling, *Historic Cottages of Mackinac Island*, Mayfield, Michigan: Arbutus Press, 2001.

Tallmadge, Thomas E. *The Story of Architecture in America*, New York: W.W. Norton and Co., 1927.

Van Fleet, Rev. J. A. *Old and New Mackinac*. Ann Arbor: Courier Steam Printing House, 1870.

White Norval. *The Architecture Book*. New York: Alfred A. Knoph, 1976.

Widder, Keith R. *Mackinac National Park, 1875-1895*. Mackinac Island: Mackinac Island State Park Commission, 1975.

Williams, Meade C. *Early Mackinac, The Fairy Island*. St. Louis: Buschart Bros., 1897.

Wood, Edwin O. *Historic Mackinac*. 2 vols. New York: MacMillan Co., 1918.

INDEX

ACKNOWLEDGEMENTS

This publication was made possible through a generous donation from the Richard and Jane Manoogian Foundation.

Chairman Dennis O. Cawthorne and the entire Mackinac Island State Park Commission are recognized for their support of this book and the entire Mackinac State Historic Parks publication program which has produced over 100 titles since 1962.

Many generous individuals assisted with the production of the second addition of *View from the Veranda*. Cindy Litzner typed the manuscript, Bill Fritz scanned the images, and Steve Brisson, Lynn Evans, Ron Crandell, and Tim Putman reviewed the manuscript and made countless corrections and improvements. Their assistance is greatly appreciated. I am also grateful to my wife Valerie and my parents Bill and Lornie Porter for their constant and encouraging support. This book is dedicated to them.